easy to make!
Wok & Stir-fry

Good Housekeeping

easy to make!
Wok & Stir-fry

COLLINS & BROWN

First published in Great Britain in 2008
by Collins & Brown
10 Southcombe Street
London W14 0RA

An imprint of Anova Books Company Ltd

The Good Housekeeping website is
www.allaboutyou.com/goodhousekeeping

10 9 8 7 6 5 4 3

ISBN 978-1-84340-465-1

A catalogue record for this book is available from the British
Library.

Reproduction by Dot Gradations Ltd
Printed and bound by Times Offset (M) Sdn. Bhd, Malaysia

This book can be ordered direct from the publisher at
www.anovabooks.com

NOTES

- Both metric and imperial measures are given for the recipes. Follow either set of measures, not a mixture of both, as they are not interchangeable.
- All spoon measures are level.
  1 tsp = 5ml spoon; 1 tbsp = 15ml spoon.
- Ovens and grills must be preheated to the specified temperature.
- Use sea salt and freshly ground black pepper unless otherwise suggested.
- Fresh herbs should be used unless dried herbs are specified in a recipe.
- Medium eggs should be used except where otherwise specified. Free-range eggs are recommended.
- Note that certain recipes, including mayonnaise, lemon curd and some cold desserts, contain raw or lightly cooked eggs. The young, elderly, pregnant women and anyone with an immune-deficiency disease should avoid these, because of the slight risk of salmonella.
- Calorie, fat and carbohydrate counts per serving are provided for the recipes.
- If you are following a gluten- or dairy-free diet, check the labels on all pre-packaged food goods.
- Recipe serving suggestions do not take gluten- or dairy-free diets into account.

Picture credits
Photographers: Martin Brigdale; Nicki Dowey (pages 38, 44, 52, 66, 86); Craig Robertson (all Basics photography); Lucinda Symons (page 76)
Stylist: Helen Trent
Home Economist: Katie Rogers

Contents

Foreword

What restaurant chefs call 'mise en place' – the French term for assembling and preparing all your ingredients before you start cooking – is more important than ever when you're using a wok. Once the oil in the pan has heated up and the ingredients start to cook, there's no turning back. Meat, fish and vegetables are tossed in the hot oil and should be cooked through but retain a firm bite. It's a great way of rustling up a quick supper – a basic stir-fry takes no more than a few minutes.

A wok can be used for far more than just stir-frying. It's a versatile pot: the deep round bowl shape means you can cook almost anything in it. Try using it for steaming: boil some water in the bottom, then pop a bamboo steamer filled with fish, chicken or vegetables on top to cook in the steam. You can also shallow- or deep-fry, braise a small piece of meat, and make some delicious soups. If you've never used a wok before, turn to the basics section, where you'll find plenty of tips to get you started.

We've gathered together 101 ways to cook in a wok, inspired by the varied cuisines of China, Japan, Indonesia and Thailand. All the recipes have been triple-tested in the Good Housekeeping kitchens to make sure they work every time for you.

Emma

Emma Marsden
Cookery Editor
Good Housekeeping

0

The Basics

Getting started

You don't need to buy special equipment to start stir-frying – a large deep-sided frying pan and a spatula will do the job – but a wok, the pan used throughout Asia, is very versatile, with many uses in the kitchen.

Choosing a wok

Traditional steel woks have rounded bottoms, so the food always returns to the centre where the heat is most intense. The deep sides prevent the food from falling out during stir-frying. Most woks now have flattened bottoms, which makes them more stable on modern hobs. Non-stick woks are widely available; they are easy to clean and not prone to rusting.

• There are two main styles of wok, one with double handles opposite each other, the other with one long handle. The double-handled wok gets very hot and needs

to be handled with oven gloves, although it is slightly more stable if you use it for steaming and braising. A wok with a long single handle is the best choice as it is easier to manipulate when stir-frying.

• A wok with a diameter of 35.5cm (14in) is most useful for cooking stir-fries for four people.

• A well-fitting lid is useful if you intend to use your wok for steaming.

Wok equipment

Wok spoon A metal utensil with a curved end to match the curve of the wok is useful for stir-frying in a traditional steel wok, but should not be used in non-stick woks – any heatproof spatula will do.

Chopsticks Long wooden chopsticks are great for stir-frying in non-stick woks; they are also useful for separating blocks of noodles as they cook.

Steamers come in various sizes, and may be of pierced metal or bamboo. They can be used in a wok or over a pan of boiling water, covered with a tight-fitting lid.

Trivet or steamer rack A wooden or metal trivet or steamer rack fits inside the wok to keep food above the water level when steaming.

Wok stand A wok stand or ring, which sits on the hob with the wok on top, helps keep the wok stable during steaming or braising.

Strainer A long-handled strainer is useful for scooping food from deep-frying oil, but a slotted spoon could be used instead.

Seasoning a wok

Non-stick woks do not need to be seasoned. Traditional steel woks, designed to withstand high temperatures, can be made practically non-stick by 'seasoning' before you use them for the first time. First scrub the wok in hot water and detergent, then dry thoroughly with kitchen paper. Place it over a low heat, add 2 tbsp groundnut oil and rub this over the entire inner surface with kitchen paper. Keep the wok over a low heat until the oil starts to smoke. Leave to cool for 5 minutes, then rub well with kitchen paper. Add another 2 tbsp oil and repeat the heating process twice more until the kitchen paper wipes clean. The wok is now seasoned. If used regularly it should remain rust-free. After each use, rinse in hot water - but not detergent - and wipe clean with kitchen paper.
If you scrub your wok or use detergent you will need to season it again.

The Asian storecupboard

Rice and noodles are the staple foods; see pages 26–7. The following items, used in many Asian dishes, are available in most large supermarkets and Asian food shops.

Spices

Chinese five-spice powder is made from star anise, fennel seeds, cinnamon, cloves and Sichuan pepper. It has a strong liquorice-like flavour and should be used sparingly.

Kaffir lime leaves, used in South-east Asian cooking for their lime-lemon flavour, are glossy leaves used whole but not eaten – rather like bay leaves. Use grated lime zest as a substitute.

Tamarind paste has a delicately sour flavour; use lemon juice as a substitute.

Sauces

Soy sauce – made from fermented soya beans and, usually, wheat – is the most common flavouring in Chinese and South-east Asian cooking. There are light and dark soy sauces; the dark kind is slightly sweeter and tends to darken the food. It will keep indefinitely.

Thai fish sauce is a salty condiment with a distinctive, pungent aroma. It is used in many South-east Asian dishes. You can buy it in most large supermarkets and Asian food stores. It will keep indefinitely.

Thai green curry paste is a blend of spices such as green chillies, coriander and lemongrass. **Thai red curry paste** contains fresh and dried red chillies and ginger. Once opened, store in a sealed container in the refrigerator for up to one month.

Chilli sauce is made from fresh red chillies, vinegar, salt and sugar; some versions include other ingredients such as garlic or ginger. Sweet chilli sauce is a useful standby for adding piquancy to all kinds of dishes.

Black bean sauce is made from fermented black beans, salt and ginger. Salty and pungent on its own, it adds richness to many stir-fry dishes.

Yellow bean sauce is a thick, salty, aromatic yellow-brown purée of fermented yellow soy beans, flour and salt.

Hoisin sauce, sometimes called barbecue sauce, is a thick, sweet-spicy red-brown sauce.

Oyster sauce is a smooth brown sauce made from oyster extract, wheat flour and other flavourings. It doesn't taste fishy, but adds a 'meaty' flavour to stir-fries and braises.

Plum sauce, made from plums, ginger, chillies, vinegar and sugar, is traditionally served with duck or as a dip.

Coconut milk

Canned coconut milk is widely available, but if you can't find it, use blocks of creamed coconut or coconut powder, following the packet instructions to make the amount of liquid you need.

Canned vegetables

Bamboo shoots, available sliced or in chunks, have a mild flavour; rinse before use.

Water chestnuts have a very mild flavour but add a lovely crunch to stir-fried and braised dishes.

Other ingredients

Dried mushrooms feature in some Chinese recipes; they need to be soaked in hot water for 30 minutes before use.

Dried shrimps and dried shrimp paste (blachan) are often used in South-east Asian cooking. The pungent smell becomes milder during cooking and marries with the other ingredients. These are often included in ready-made sauces and spice pastes, and are not suitable for vegetarians.

Mirin is a sweet rice wine from Japan; if you can't find it, use dry or medium sherry instead.

Rice wine is often used in Chinese cooking; if you can't find it, use dry sherry instead.

Rice vinegar is clear and milder than other vinegars. Use white wine vinegar or cider vinegar as a substitute.

Which oil to use?

Groundnut (peanut) oil has a mild flavour and is widely used in China and South-east Asia. It is well suited to stir-frying and deep-frying as it has a high smoke point and can therefore be used at high temperatures.

Vegetable oil may be pure rapeseed oil, or a blend of corn, soya bean, rapeseed or other oils. It usually has a bland flavour and is suitable for stir-frying.

Sesame oil has a distinctive nutty flavour; it is best used in marinades or added as a seasoning to stir-fried dishes just before serving.

Stir-frying

Stir-fries can be as simple or as substantial as you feel like making them. It's a quick cooking method – but you need to have all the ingredients prepared before you start cooking. If you buy ready-prepared stir-fry vegetables, a meal can be on the table in minutes. Ensure your wok or pan is very hot before you start cooking and keep the ingredients moving so they don't stick or burn.

Stir-frying vegetables

Stir-frying is perfect for non-starchy vegetables, as the quick cooking preserves their colour, freshness and texture.

To serve four, you will need:
450g (1lb) vegetables, 1–2 tbsp vegetable oil, 2 crushed garlic cloves, 2 tbsp soy sauce, 2 tsp sesame oil.

1 Cut the vegetables into even-sized pieces. Heat the vegetable oil in a large wok or frying pan until smoking-hot. Add the garlic and cook for a few seconds, then remove and set aside.

2 Add the vegetables to the wok, and toss and stir them. Keep them moving constantly as they cook, which will take 4–5 minutes.

3 When the vegetables are just tender, but still with a slight bite, turn off the heat. Put the garlic back into the wok and stir well. Add the soy sauce and sesame oil, toss and serve.

Perfect stir-frying

Cut everything into small pieces of similar size, shape and thickness so that they cook quickly and evenly.
If you're cooking onions or garlic with the vegetables, don't keep them over the high heat for too long or they will burn.
Add liquids towards the end of cooking so that they don't evaporate.

Stir-frying fish and shellfish

Use shellfish or a firm fish such as monkfish, as more delicate fish will break up.

1 Cut into bite-size pieces. Heat a wok or large pan until very hot and add oil to coat the inside.

2 Add the fish and toss over a high heat for 2 minutes until just cooked. Remove and put to one side. Cook the other stir-fry ingredients. Return the fish to the wok or pan for 1 minute to heat through.

Stir-frying poultry and meat

Stir-frying is ideal for poultry and tender cuts of meat.

1 Trim off any fat, then cut the poultry or meat into even-sized strips or dice no more than 5mm ($^1\!/_4$ in) thick. Heat a wok or large pan until hot and add oil to coat the inside.

2 Add the poultry or meat and cook, stirring constantly, until just done. Remove and put to one side. Cook the other ingredients you are using for the stir-fry, then return the poultry or meat to the pan and cook for 1–2 minutes to heat through.

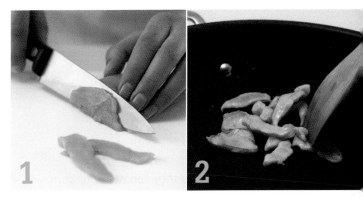

Health Tip

Stir-frying in a wok uses less fat than other frying techniques, and cooking briefly over a high heat retains as many nutrients as possible.

Steaming, braising and deep-frying

These three cooking techniques show the versatility of the wok. It can also be used for blanching vegetables, lightly toasting nuts, seeds and spices, or even sautéing potatoes.

Steaming

To use your wok as a steamer you will need a trivet or steamer rack to place inside the wok. The steamer basket (metal or bamboo) sits on the trivet to keep the food above the boiling liquid. Steaming is ideal for fish, chicken and most vegetables.

1 Put the fish or chicken on a lightly oiled heatproof plate that will fit inside the steamer. (Vegetables can be placed directly on the steamer.)

2 Bring the water in the wok or pan to the boil over a medium heat. Put the plate with the fish or chicken in the steamer, cover with a tight-fitting lid and steam until just cooked through (see chart, right).

Health Tip

Steaming allows food to retain maximum flavour and colour, as well as the vitamins that are easily lost during boiling or poaching.

Marinades

If you like, marinate fish or chicken before steaming, in a mixture of vegetable oil, soy sauce and sliced garlic or ginger.

- Fish needs only 10 minutes marinating before steaming.
- If you are steaming a whole fish, slash the skin diagonally on both sides so the marinade can penetrate the flesh. This also helps the fish to cook more quickly.

Deep-frying

Shellfish and small pieces of fish, carrots, broccoli, onions, courgettes, aubergines, mushrooms, peppers and cauliflower are all good deep-fried in a light batter.

To serve four, you will need:
About 900g (2lb) mixed vegetables (such as aubergines, broccoli, cauliflower, red peppers), cut into small, similar-sized pieces, 125g (4oz) plain flour, 125g (4oz) cornflour, a pinch of salt, 1 medium egg yolk, 300ml (½ pint) sparkling water.

1 Prepare the vegetables and cut into small pieces (no more than 2cm (¾in) thick). Dry well on kitchen paper.

2 Heat vegetable oil in a deep-fryer to 170°C (a small cube of bread should brown in 40 seconds).

3 To make the batter, lightly whisk together the flour, cornflour, salt, egg yolk and water.

4 Coat the vegetables lightly with flour, then dip into the batter.

5 Fry in batches, a few pieces at a time, until the batter is crisp and golden brown. Don't put too many vegetables in the pan at once (if you do, the temperature drops and the vegetables take longer to cook and become greasy). Remove with a slotted spoon and drain on kitchen paper before serving.

5

Braising

Braising in a wok is not the same as European-style braising. It's generally a much quicker process: the ingredients are cut small and usually stir-fried first, then covered with liquid such as stock or coconut milk and simmered until just tender.

Steaming times

Leafy vegetables such as spinach, Chinese leaves	1–2 minutes
Vegetables such as green beans, broccoli, cauliflower, cabbage, carrots	5–8 minutes
Fish fillet	5–10 minutes (allow 10 minutes per 2.5cm (1in) thickness)
Fish steaks and whole fish	15–20 minutes
Chicken	45–50 minutes (depending on whether chicken is shredded, cubed, boned thighs or halved breasts)

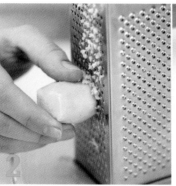

Ginger

1 **Grating** Cut off a piece of the root and peel with a vegetable peeler. Cut off any brown spots.

2 Rest the grater on a board or small plate and grate the ginger. Discard any large fibres adhering to the pulp.

3 **Slicing, shredding and chopping** Cut slices off the ginger and cut off the skin carefully. Cut off any brown spots. Stack the slices and cut into shreds. To chop, stack the shreds and cut across into small pieces.

4 **Pressing** If you just need the ginger juice, peel and cut off any brown spots, then cut into small chunks and use a garlic press held over a small bowl to extract the juice.

Flavourings

Many stir-fry recipes begin by cooking garlic, ginger and spring onions as the basic flavourings. Spicier dishes may include chillies, lemongrass or a prepared spice paste such as Thai curry paste.

Spring onions

Cut off the roots and trim any coarse or withered green parts. Slice diagonally, or shred by cutting into 5cm (2in) lengths then slicing down the lengths, or chop finely, according to the recipe.

Garlic

1 Put the clove on a chopping board and place the flat side of a large knife on top of it. Press down firmly on the flat of the blade to crush the clove and break the papery skin.

2 Cut off the base of the clove and slip the garlic out of its skin. It should come away easily.

3 **Slicing** Using a rocking motion with the knife tip on the board, slice the garlic as thinly as you need.

4 **Shredding and chopping** Holding the slices together, shred them across the slices. Chop the shreds if you need chopped garlic.

5 **Crushing** After step 2, the whole clove can be put into a garlic press. To crush with a knife: roughly chop the peeled cloves with a pinch of salt. Press down hard with the edge of a large knife tip (with the blade facing away from you), then drag the blade along the garlic while still pressing hard. Continue to do this, dragging the knife tip over the garlic.

Chillies

1 Cut off the cap and slit open lengthways. Using a spoon, scrape out the seeds and the pith.

2 For diced chilli, cut into thin shreds lengthways, then cut crossways.

Cook's Tip

Wash hands thoroughly after handling chillies – the volatile oils will sting if accidentally rubbed into your eyes.

Coriander

Coriander, also known as Chinese parsley, is the most commonly used herb throughout Asia. In Thailand the roots are often used in curry pastes.

1 Trim off any roots and the lower part of the stalks. Immerse in cold water and shake briskly. Leave in the water for a few minutes.

2 Lift out of the water and put in a colander or sieve, then rinse again under the cold tap. Leave to drain for a few minutes, then dry thoroughly on kitchen paper or teatowels, or use a salad spinner.
Note: Don't pour the herbs and their water into the sieve, because dirt in the water might get caught in the leaves.

3 Gather the leaves into a compact ball in one hand, keeping your fist around the ball (but being careful not to crush them). Chop with a large knife, using a rocking motion and letting just a little of the ball out of your fingers at a time.

4 When the herbs are roughly chopped, continue chopping until the pieces are as fine as you need.

Lemongrass

Lemongrass is a popular South-east Asian ingredient, giving an aromatic lemony flavour. It looks rather like a long, slender spring onion, but is fibrous and woody and is usually removed before the dish is served. Alternatively the inner leaves may be very finely chopped or pounded in a mortar and pestle and used in spice pastes.

Onions

1 Cut off the tip and base of the onion. Peel away all the layers of papery skin and any discoloured layers underneath.

2 Put the onion root end down on the chopping board, then, using a sharp knife, cut the onion in half from tip to base.

3 **Slicing** Put one half on the board with the cut surface facing down and slice across the onion.

4 **Chopping** Slice the halved onions from the root end to the top at regular intervals. Next, make two or three horizontal slices through the onion, then slice vertically across the width.

Preparing vegetables

A few basic techniques will help you prepare all kinds of vegetables ready for quick cooking in the wok. For a meal in minutes, look for bags of ready-prepared stir-fry vegetables.

Leeks

As some leeks harbour a lot of grit and earth between their leaves, they need careful cleaning.

1 Cut off the root and any tough parts of the leek. Make a cut into the leaf end of the leek, about 7.5cm (3in) deep.

2 Hold under the cold tap while separating the cut halves to expose any grit. Wash well, then shake dry. Slice, cut into matchsticks or slice diagonally.

Pak choi

Also known as bok choy, pak choi is a type of cabbage that does not form a heart. It has dark green leaves and thick fleshy white stalks, which are sometimes cooked separately.

Cabbage

The crinkly-leaved Savoy cabbage may need more washing than other varieties, because its open leaves catch dirt more easily than the tightly packed white and red cabbage. The following method is suitable for all cabbages, including mild-flavoured Chinese leaves or Chinese cabbage.

1 Pick off any of the outer leaves that are dry, tough or discoloured. Cut off the base and, using a small sharp knife, cut out as much as possible of the tough inner core in a single cone-shaped piece.

2 If you need whole cabbage leaves, peel them off one by one. As you work your way down, you will need to cut out more of the core.

3 If you are cooking the cabbage in wedges, cut it in half lengthways, then cut the pieces into wedges of the required size.

Shredding cabbage

Cut the cabbage into quarters, then slice with a large cook's knife. Alternatively, use the shredding disc of a food processor.

Broccoli

1 Slice off the end of the stalk and cut 1cm (½in) below the florets. Cut the broccoli head in half.

2 Peel the thick, woody skin from the stalks and slice the stalks in half or quarters lengthways. Cut off equal-sized florets with a small knife. If the florets are very large, or if you want them for a stir-fry, you can halve them by cutting lengthways through the stalk and pulling the two halves apart.

Courgettes

Cutting diagonally is ideal for courgettes and other vegetables in a stir-fry.

Carrots

1 **Paring ribbons** Cut off the ends, then, using a vegetable peeler, peel off the skin and discard. Continue peeling the carrot into ribbon strips.

2 **Slicing** Cut slices off each of the rounded sides to make four flat surfaces that are stable on the chopping board. Hold steady with one hand and cut lengthways into even slices so they are lying in a flat stack. The stack can then be cut into batons or matchsticks.

Asparagus

Cut the asparagus spears about 5cm (2in) from the stalk end, or where the white and green sections meet. Or snap off the woody tip of the stem; it will snap just where the stem becomes tender. Discard the woody end.

Perfect vegetables

Wash vegetables before you cut them up, to retain as many nutrients as possible.

Cook as soon as possible after you have cut them.

Do not overcook vegetables or they will lose their bright colour, crisp texture and some of their nutrients.

Peppers

Red, green and yellow peppers all contain seeds and white pith which taste bitter and should be removed. **Cut** the pepper in half vertically, discard the seeds and core, then trim away the rest of the white membrane with a small sharp knife. Alternatively, slice the top off the pepper, then cut away and discard the seeds and pith. Cut the pepper into strips or slices.

Celery

To remove the strings in the outer green stalks, trim the ends and cut into the base of the stalk with a small knife; catch the strings between the blade and your thumb. Pull up towards the top of the stalk to remove the string.

Mushrooms

Button, white, chestnut and flat mushrooms are all prepared in a similar way.
Shiitake mushrooms have a hard stalk; cut it off and use for making stock if you like.

1   Wipe with a damp cloth or pastry brush to remove any dirt.

2   With button mushrooms, cut off the stalk flush with the base of the cap. For other mushrooms, cut a thin disc off the end of the stalk and discard. Quarter or slice as needed.

Fennel

1   Trim off the top stems and the base of the bulbs. Remove the core with a small sharp knife if it is tough.

2   The outer leaves may be discoloured and can be scrubbed gently in cold water, or you can peel away the discoloured parts with a knife or a vegetable peeler. Slice or chop the fennel.

Sprouting beans

You will only need about 3 tbsp beans to sprout at one time.

1 Pick through the beans to remove any grit or stones, then soak in cold water for at least 8 hours. Drain and place in a clean (preferably sterilised) jar. Cover the top with a dampened piece of clean cloth, secure and leave in a warm, dark place.

2 Rinse the sprouting beans twice a day. The sprouts can be eaten when there is about 1cm ($\frac{1}{2}$in) of growth, or they can be left to grow for a day or two longer. When they are sprouted, leave the jar on a sunny windowsill for about 3 hours – this will improve both their flavour and their nutrients. Then rinse and dry them well. They can be kept for about three days in the refrigerator.

Growing your own sprouted beans

Mung beans are the most commonly used sprouted beans for stir-fries, but chickpeas, green or Puy lentils and alfalfa are equally good and easy for home sprouting.

Cook's Tips

Use only fresh bean sprouts; when buying, look for plump, crisp white shoots; avoid those that feel limp or are starting to brown.
Store bean sprouts in a plastic bag in the refrigerator for up to two days.
Rinse in ice-cold water and drain well before use.

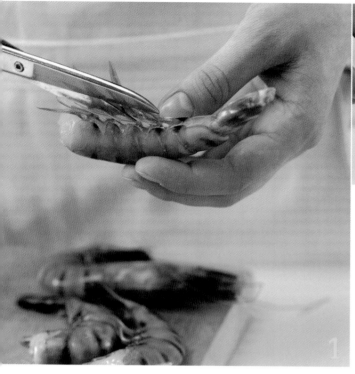

Preparing shellfish

Prawns, mussels and small squid are ideal for stir-frying and quick braising, because they need very brief cooking, otherwise they will become rubbery.

Prawns

Prawns are delicious stir-fried. They can be completely shelled, or you can leave the tail on, but they should be deveined before using.

1 Pull off the head and discard (or put to one side and use later for making stock). Using pointed scissors, cut through the soft shell on the belly side.

2 Prise the shell off, leaving the tail attached. (The shell can also be used later for making stock.)

3 Using a small sharp knife, make a shallow cut along the back of the prawn. Using the point of the knife, remove and discard the black vein (the intestinal tract) that runs along the back of the prawn.

Mussels

Mussels take moments to cook, but careful preparation is important, so give yourself enough time to get the shellfish ready.

1 Scrape off the fibres attached to the shells (beards). If the mussels are very clean, give them a quick rinse under the cold tap. If they are very sandy, scrub them with a stiff brush.

2 If the shells have sizeable barnacles on them, it's best (though not essential) to remove them. Rap them sharply with a metal spoon or the back of a washing-up brush, then scrape off.

3 Discard any open mussels that don't shut when sharply tapped; this means they are dead and may lead to food poisoning.

Squid

Sliced into rings or cut into squares, squid is a popular fish in Chinese and South-east Asian cooking.

1 Cut off the tentacles just behind the 'beak'.

2 Pull out the beak and discard. Clean the tentacles well, scraping off as many of the small suckers as you can.

3 Reach inside the body and pull out the internal organs, including the plastic-like 'pen'.

4 Scrape and pull off the loose, slippery skin covering the body. Rinse the body thoroughly to remove all internal organs, sand and other debris.

5 Detach the wings and set aside, then cut up the tentacles and body as required. To make squares, slice the body along one side, score diagonally, then cut into squares.

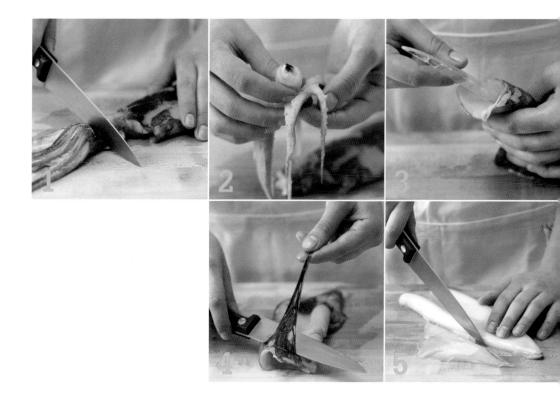

Cooking rice

There are two main types of rice: long-grain and short-grain. Long-grain rice is generally served as an accompaniment; the most commonly used type of long-grain rice in South-east Asian cooking is jasmine rice, also known as Thai fragrant rice. It has a distinctive taste and slightly sticky texture. Long-grain rice needs no special preparation, although it should be washed to remove excess starch. Put the rice in a bowl and cover with cold water. Stir until this becomes cloudy, then drain and repeat until the water is clear.

Long-grain rice

1 Use 50–75g (2–3oz) raw rice per person; measured by volume 50–75ml (2–2½fl oz). Measure the rice by volume and put it in a pan with a pinch of salt and twice the volume of boiling water (or stock).

2 Bring to the boil. Turn the heat down to low and set the timer for the time stated on the pack. The rice should be al dente: tender with a bite at the centre.

3 When the rice is cooked, fluff up the grains with a fork.

Cooking rice and noodles

Rice and noodles are the staples of Asian cooking. Often served as an accompaniment to stir-fried dishes, they can also be cooked and added as one of the ingredients.

Perfect rice

Use 50–75g (2–3oz) raw rice per person – or measure by volume 50–75ml (2–2½fl oz).
If you cook rice often, you may want to invest in a special rice steamer. They are available in Asian supermarkets and some kitchen shops and give good, consistent results.

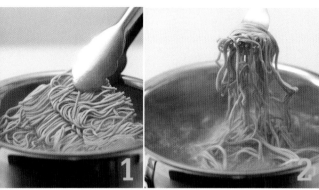

Cooking noodles

Egg (wheat) noodles

These are the most versatile of Asian noodles. Like Italian pasta, they are made from wheat flour, egg and water and are available fresh or dried in various thicknesses.

1 Bring a pan of water to the boil and put the noodles in.

2 Agitate the noodles using chopsticks or a fork to separate them. This can take a minute or even more.

3 Continue boiling for 4–5 minutes until the noodles are cooked al dente: tender but with a little bite in the centre.

4 Drain well and then rinse in cold water and toss with a little oil if you are not using them immediately.

Glass, cellophane or bean thread noodles

These very thin noodles are made from mung beans; they need only 1 minute in boiling water.

Rice noodles

These may be very fine (rice vermicelli) or thick and flat. Most need no cooking, only soaking in warm or hot water; check the packet instructions, or cover the noodles with freshly boiled water and soak until they are al dente: tender but with a little bite in the centre. Drain well and toss with a little oil if you are not using them immediately.

Perfect noodles

Use 50–75g (2–3oz) uncooked noodles per person.
Dried egg noodles are often packed in layers. As a general rule, allow one layer per person for a main dish.
If you plan to re-cook the noodles after the initial boiling or soaking – for example, in a stir-fry – it's best to undercook them slightly.
When cooking a layer, block or nest of noodles, use a pair of forks or chopsticks to untangle the strands from the moment they go into the water.

Food storage and hygiene

Storing food properly and preparing it in a hygienic way is important to ensure that food remains as nutritious and flavourful as possible, and to reduce the risk of food poisoning.

Hygiene

When you are preparing food, always follow these important guidelines:

Wash your hands thoroughly before handling food and again between handling different types of food, such as raw and cooked meat and poultry. If you have any cuts or grazes on your hands, be sure to keep them covered with a waterproof plaster.

Wash down worksurfaces regularly with a mild detergent solution or multi-surface cleaner.

Use a dishwasher if available. Otherwise, wear rubber gloves for washing-up, so that the water temperature can be hotter than unprotected hands can bear. Change drying-up cloths and cleaning cloths regularly. Note that leaving dishes to drain is more hygienic than drying them with a teatowel.

Keep raw and cooked foods separate, especially meat, fish and poultry. Wash kitchen utensils in between preparing raw and cooked foods. Never put cooked or ready-to-eat foods directly on to a surface which has just had raw fish, meat or poultry on it.

Keep pets out of the kitchen if possible; or make sure they stay away from worksurfaces. Never allow animals on to worksurfaces.

Shopping

Always choose fresh ingredients in prime condition from stores and markets that have a regular turnover of stock to ensure you buy the freshest produce possible.

Make sure items are within their 'best before' or 'use by' date. (Foods with a longer shelf life have a 'best before' date; more perishable items have a 'use by' date.)

Pack frozen and chilled items in an insulated cool bag at the check-out and put them into the freezer or refrigerator as soon as you get home.

During warm weather in particular, buy perishable foods just before you return home. When packing items at the check-out, sort them according to where you will store them when you get home – the refrigerator, freezer, storecupboard, vegetable rack, fruit bowl, etc. This will make unpacking easier – and quicker.

The storecupboard

Although storecupboard ingredients will generally last a long time, correct storage is important:

Always check packaging for storage advice – even with familiar foods, because storage requirements may change if additives, sugar or salt have been reduced. Check storecupboard foods for their 'best before' or 'use by' date and do not use them if the date has passed.

Keep all food cupboards scrupulously clean and make sure food containers and packets are properly sealed.

Once opened, treat canned foods as though fresh. Always transfer the contents to a clean container, cover and keep in the refrigerator. Similarly, jars, sauce bottles and cartons should be kept chilled after opening. (Check the label for safe storage times after opening.)

Transfer dry goods such as sugar, rice and pasta to moisture-proof containers. When supplies are used up, wash the container well and thoroughly dry before refilling with new supplies.

Store oils in a dark cupboard away from any heat source as heat and light can make them turn rancid and affect their colour. For the same reason, buy olive oil in dark green bottles.

Store vinegars in a cool place; they can turn bad in a warm environment.

Store dried herbs, spices and flavourings in a cool, dark cupboard or in dark jars. Buy in small quantities as their flavour will not last indefinitely.

Store flours and sugars in airtight containers.

Refrigerator storage

Fresh food needs to be kept in the cool temperature of the refrigerator to keep it in good condition and discourage the growth of harmful bacteria. Store day-to-day perishable items, such as opened jams and jellies, mayonnaise and bottled sauces, in the refrigerator along with eggs and dairy products, fruit juices, bacon, fresh and cooked meat (on separate shelves), and salads and vegetables (except potatoes, which don't suit being stored in the cold). A refrigerator should be kept at an operating temperature of 4–5°C. It is worth investing in a refrigerator thermometer to ensure the correct temperature is maintained.

To ensure your refrigerator is functioning effectively for safe food storage, follow these guidelines:

To avoid bacterial cross-contamination, store cooked and raw foods on separate shelves, putting cooked foods on the top shelf. Ensure that all items are well wrapped.

Never put hot food into the refrigerator, as this will cause the internal temperature of the refrigerator to rise.

Avoid overfilling the refrigerator, as this restricts the circulation of air and prevents the appliance from working properly.

It can take some time for the refrigerator to return to the correct operating temperature once the door has been opened, so don't leave it open any longer than is necessary.

Clean the refrigerator regularly, using a specially formulated germicidal refrigerator cleaner. Alternatively, use a weak solution of bicarbonate of soda: 1 tbsp to 1 litre (1³/₄ pints) water.

If your refrigerator doesn't have an automatic defrost facility, defrost regularly.

Maximum refrigerator storage times

For pre-packed foods, always adhere to the 'use by' date on the packet. For other foods the following storage times should apply, providing the food is in prime condition when it goes into the refrigerator and that your refrigerator is in good working order:

Vegetables

Green vegetables	3–4 days
Salad leaves	2–3 days

Dairy Food

Eggs	1 week
Milk	4–5 days

Fish

Fish	1 day
Shellfish	1 day

Raw Meat

Bacon	7 days
Game	2 days
Minced meat	1 day
Offal	1 day
Poultry	2 days
Raw sliced meat	2 days

Cooked Meat

Sliced meat	2 days
Ham	2 days
Ham, vacuum-packed (or according to the instructions on the packet)	1–2 weeks

1

Fish and Shellfish

Try Something Different

Instead of prawns, try chicken cut into strips; stir-fry for 5 minutes in step 1.

Five-minute Stir-fry

1 tbsp sesame oil

175g (6oz) raw peeled tiger prawns, deveined

50ml (2fl oz) ready-made sweet chilli and ginger sauce

225g (8oz) ready-prepared mixed stir-fry vegetables, such as sliced courgettes, broccoli and green beans

1 Heat the oil in a large wok or frying pan, add the prawns and sweet chilli and ginger sauce and stir-fry for 2 minutes.

2 Add the mixed vegetables and stir-fry for a further 2–3 minutes until the prawns are cooked and the vegetables are heated through. Serve immediately.

Serves	EASY		NUTRITIONAL INFORMATION	
2	**Preparation Time** 2 minutes	**Cooking Time** 5 minutes	**Per Serving** 170 calories, 7g fat (of which 1g saturates), 11g carbohydrate, 1.6g salt	Gluten free • Dairy free

2 tbsp vegetable oil

500g (1lb 2oz) shelled large scallops,
cut into 5mm (¼ in) slices

4 celery sticks, sliced diagonally

1 bunch of spring onions, sliced diagonally

25g (1oz) piece fresh root ginger, peeled and sliced

2 large garlic cloves, sliced

¼ tsp chilli powder

2 tbsp lemon juice

2 tbsp light soy sauce

3 tbsp freshly chopped coriander

salt and ground black pepper

Scallops with Ginger

1 Heat the oil in a wok or large frying pan. Add the scallops, celery, spring onions, ginger, garlic and chilli powder and stir-fry over a high heat for 2 minutes or until the vegetables are just tender.

2 Pour in the lemon juice and soy sauce, allow to bubble up, then stir in about 2 tbsp chopped coriander and season with salt and pepper. Serve immediately, sprinkled with the remaining coriander.

EASY		NUTRITIONAL INFORMATION		Serves
Preparation Time 15 minutes	**Cooking Time** 3 minutes	**Per Serving** 197 calories, 7g fat (of which 1g saturates), 6g carbohydrate, 2g salt	Dairy free	**4**

Thai Coconut Mussels

1 tbsp vegetable oil

2 shallots, finely chopped

2–3 tbsp Thai green curry paste

400ml can coconut milk

2kg (4½lb) mussels, scrubbed and beards removed

a small handful of coriander, chopped, plus extra sprigs to garnish

1 Heat the oil in a large, deep pan. Add the shallots and curry paste and fry gently for 5 minutes, stirring regularly, until the shallots are starting to soften. Stir in the coconut milk, cover with a tight-fitting lid and bring to the boil.

2 Add the mussels to the pan, cover, shake the pan well and cook over a medium heat for 4–5 minutes. Give the pan another good shake. Check the mussels and discard any that are still closed. Stir in the chopped coriander and serve immediately, garnished with coriander sprigs.

Try Something Different

Instead of mussels you could use 500g (1lb 2oz) large raw peeled prawns; simmer for 5 minutes until the prawns are cooked and pink.

EASY		NUTRITIONAL INFORMATION		Serves
Preparation Time 15 minutes	**Cooking Time** about 12 minutes	**Per Serving** 210 calories, 7g fat (of which 1g saturates), 13g carbohydrate, 1.6g salt	Gluten free • Dairy free	**4**

Cook's Tips

Chillies vary enormously in strength, from quite mild to blisteringly hot, depending on the type of chilli and its ripeness. Taste a small piece first to check it's not too hot for you.

Be extremely careful when handling chillies not to touch or rub your eyes with your fingers, as they will sting. Wash knives immediately after handling chillies for the same reason. As a precaution, use rubber gloves when preparing them if you like.

As a general rule, the smaller the chilli, the hotter it is.

Asparagus with Crab and Pineapple

75g (3oz) Thai fragrant rice, rinsed and drained

2 tbsp sunflower oil

2 small green chillies, seeded and finely chopped (see Cook's Tip)

2 garlic cloves, finely chopped

4 spring onions, finely chopped

1 tsp paprika

$\frac{1}{2}$ tsp ground coriander

$\frac{1}{4}$ tsp cayenne pepper

225g (8oz) thin asparagus spears, cut into short lengths

150g (5oz) white crab meat, thawed if frozen

2 medium eggs, beaten

125g (4oz) fresh pineapple slices, cored and cut into chunks

1 tbsp Thai fish sauce

1 tbsp lime juice

salt and ground black pepper

lime wedges to serve

1 Cook the rice for 10 minutes or according to the packet instructions.

2 When the rice has been cooking for 5 minutes, heat the oil in a wok or large frying pan, add the chillies, garlic, spring onions and spices and fry over a low heat for 5 minutes. Increase the heat and add the asparagus. Stir-fry for 2 minutes, then add the cooked rice and crab meat and stir-fry for a further 2–3 minutes.

3 Add the eggs to the pan and stir over a high heat for 2–3 minutes until just set. Add the pineapple chunks, fish sauce and lime juice. Cover and cook for 5 minutes until heated through.

4 Season with salt and pepper, then serve immediately with lime wedges for squeezing over.

Serves 4	EASY		NUTRITIONAL INFORMATION	
	Preparation Time 15 minutes	**Cooking Time** about 20 minutes	**Per Serving** 237 calories, 9g fat (of which 2g saturates), 30g carbohydrate, 0.8g salt	Gluten free • Dairy free

Cook's Tip

If raw prawns are difficult to find, use cooked ones instead. Add them to the sauce and heat through for 2–3 minutes – no longer or they will become rubbery.

Prawns and Cucumber in a Spicy Sauce

2 medium cucumbers, halved lengthways, seeded and cut into 2.5cm (1in) chunks

50g (2oz) butter

2 onions, sliced

2 garlic cloves, finely chopped

4 tsp plain flour

2 tsp ground turmeric

1 tsp ground cinnamon

2 tsp sugar

½ tsp ground cloves

750ml (1¼ pints) coconut milk

300ml (½ pint) fish stock

15g (½oz) fresh root ginger, peeled and thinly sliced

3–4 green chillies, thinly sliced (see page 36)

450g (1lb) raw tiger prawns, peeled and deveined

grated zest and juice of 1 lime

2 tbsp freshly chopped coriander

salt

1 Put the cucumber in a colander set over a bowl and sprinkle with salt. Leave for 30 minutes, to allow the salt to extract the excess juices.

2 Melt the butter in a pan, add the onions and garlic and cook for about 5 minutes until softened. Add the flour, turmeric, cinnamon, 1 tsp salt, the sugar and cloves; cook, stirring, for 2 minutes. Add the coconut milk and fish stock, bring to the boil and simmer for 5 minutes.

3 Meanwhile, rinse the cucumber thoroughly under cold running water to remove the salt. Add the cucumber, ginger and chillies to the sauce, and cook for a further 10 minutes.

4 Add the prawns to the sauce and cook for a further 5–6 minutes until they turn pink.

5 Just before serving, stir in the lime juice and chopped coriander and sprinkle with lime zest.

EASY		NUTRITIONAL INFORMATION	Serves
Preparation Time 20 minutes, plus standing	**Cooking Time** 30 minutes	**Per Serving** 273 calories, 13g fat (of which 7g saturates), 27g carbohydrate, 2.5g salt	**4**

Cook's Tip

Chinese mustard cabbage, otherwise called mustard greens, is a green or red Oriental leaf that has a mild mustard flavour.

Stir-fried Prawns with Cabbage

2 tbsp vegetable oil

2 garlic cloves, thinly sliced

1 lemongrass stalk, halved and bruised

2 kaffir lime leaves, finely torn

1 small red onion, thinly sliced

1 hot red chilli, seeded and sliced (see page 36)

4cm (1½in) piece fresh root ginger, peeled and cut into long thin shreds

1 tbsp coriander seeds, lightly crushed

450g (1lb) large raw peeled prawns, deveined

175g (6oz) mangetouts, halved

225g (8oz) pak choi or Chinese mustard cabbage (see Cook's Tip), torn into bite-size pieces

2 tbsp Thai fish sauce

juice of 1 lime, or to taste

1 Heat the oil in a wok or large frying pan. Add the garlic, lemongrass, lime leaves, onion, chilli, ginger and coriander seeds, and stir-fry for 2 minutes.

2 Add the prawns, mangetouts and pak choi or cabbage, and stir-fry until the vegetables are cooked but still crisp and the prawns are pink and opaque, about 2–3 minutes.

3 Add the fish sauce and lime juice and cook for 1 minute until heated through. Remove the lemongrass and discard; serve immediately.

Serves 4	EASY		NUTRITIONAL INFORMATION	
	Preparation Time 30 minutes	**Cooking Time** 5–7 minutes	**Per Serving** 193 calories, 8g fat (of which 1g saturates), 7g carbohydrate, 1.4g salt	Gluten free • Dairy free

Cook's Tip

In Thailand, this might be made with tiny pea aubergines – look out for them in Thai food shops.

Thai Curry with Prawns and Aubergines

1 tbsp vegetable oil

1 onion, thinly sliced

250g (9oz) baby aubergines, halved lengthways

1–2 tbsp Thai red curry paste

400ml can coconut milk

200ml (7fl oz) hot fish stock

1 tbsp Thai fish sauce (optional)

200g (7oz) raw peeled tiger prawns, deveined

3 tbsp fresh coriander, roughly chopped, plus extra sprigs to garnish

salt and ground black pepper

1 Heat the oil in a wok or large frying pan. Add the onion and fry over a medium heat until golden. Add the aubergines and fry for a further 5 minutes until pale brown.

2 Add the curry paste and stir to coat the vegetables, then continue to cook for 1 minute.

3 Add the coconut milk, stock and fish sauce, if using, then bring to the boil and simmer for 5 minutes.

4 Add the prawns and season generously with salt and pepper. Simmer until the prawns have turned pink – a couple of minutes.

5 Stir in the coriander, then transfer to four large warmed serving bowls and serve immediately, garnished with coriander sprigs.

EASY		NUTRITIONAL INFORMATION		Serves
Preparation Time 10 minutes	**Cooking Time** 20 minutes	**Per Serving** 101 calories, 4g fat (of which 1g saturates), 5g carbohydrate, 0.4g salt	Gluten free • Dairy free	**4**

Squid and Vegetables in Black Bean Sauce

450g (1lb) cleaned squid
2 tbsp sesame seeds
2 tbsp sunflower oil
1 tbsp sesame oil
2 garlic cloves
2 dried red chillies
50g (2oz) broccoli, cut into florets
50g (2oz) mangetouts, trimmed
50g (2oz) carrots, thinly sliced
75g (3oz) cauliflower, cut into small florets
1 small green or red pepper, seeded and thinly sliced
50g (2oz) Chinese cabbage or pak choi, shredded
25g (1oz) bean sprouts
2 tbsp fresh coriander, roughly torn

For the sauce

2 tbsp black bean sauce
1 tbsp Thai fish sauce
2–3 tsp clear honey
75ml (2½fl oz) fish or vegetable stock
1 tbsp tamarind juice
2 tsp cornflour

1 First, prepare the sauce. In a small bowl, mix together the black bean sauce, fish sauce, honey and stock. Add the tamarind juice and cornflour and whisk until smooth. Set aside.

2 Wash and dry the squid, and halve the tentacles if large. Open out the body pouches, score diagonally, then cut into large squares; set aside.

3 Toast the sesame seeds in a dry wok or large frying pan over a medium heat, stirring until they turn golden. Tip on to a plate.

4 Heat the sunflower and sesame oil in the same pan. Add the garlic and chillies and fry gently for 5 minutes. Remove the garlic and chillies with a slotted spoon and discard.

5 Add all the vegetables to the pan and stir-fry for 3 minutes. Add the squid, increase the heat and stir-fry for a further 2 minutes until the squid curls up and turns opaque. Add the sauce and allow to simmer for 1 minute.

6 Scatter over the sesame seeds and coriander and serve immediately.

Try Something Different

Instead of squid, try 400g (14oz) rump steak, cut into thin strips.

Serves 4	A LITTLE EFFORT		NUTRITIONAL INFORMATION	
	Preparation Time 35 minutes	**Cooking Time** 10–15 minutes	**Per Serving** 274 calories, 15g fat (of which 2g saturates), 12g carbohydrate, 1g salt	Gluten free • Dairy free

Cook's Tip

When trimming okra, snip only a tiny piece from each end. Avoid cutting into the flesh or the okra will become sticky and soggy during cooking.

3 tbsp ghee or vegetable oil

2 red onions, thinly sliced

700g (1½lb) large raw prawns, peeled and deveined

450g (1lb) fresh small okra, trimmed

2 small green chillies, sliced (see page 36)

1 garlic clove (optional), sliced

2 tsp ground cumin

1 tbsp mustard seeds

3 medium ripe juicy tomatoes, cut into small wedges

squeeze of lemon juice to taste

2 tsp garam masala

3 tbsp coarsely grated fresh coconut or desiccated coconut, toasted

salt and ground black pepper

Prawns with Okra

1 Heat the ghee or oil in a wok or large heavy-based frying pan. Add the onions and cook over a high heat until browned. Add the prawns, okra, chillies, garlic if using, ground cumin and mustard seeds. Cook over a high heat, shaking the pan constantly, for 5 minutes or until the prawns are bright pink and the okra is softened but not soggy.

2 Add the tomato wedges and salt and pepper to taste. Cook for 1–2 minutes until heated through; the tomatoes should retain their shape. Add a little lemon juice to taste.

3 Tip the mixture into a serving dish and sprinkle with the garam masala and coconut. Serve immediately.

Serves 4	EASY		NUTRITIONAL INFORMATION	
	Preparation Time 25 minutes	**Cooking Time** 10 minutes	**Per Serving** 215 calories, 12g fat (of which 1.6g saturates), 5g carbohydrate, 0.5g salt	Gluten free • Dairy free

Cook's Tip

If you can't find half-fat coconut milk, use half a can of full-fat coconut milk and make up the difference with water or stock. Freeze the remaining milk for up to one month.

Thai Red Seafood Curry

1 tbsp vegetable oil

3 tbsp Thai red curry paste

450g (1lb) monkfish tail, boned to make 350g (12oz) fillet, sliced into rounds

350g (12oz) large raw peeled prawns, deveined

400ml can half-fat coconut milk

200ml (7fl oz) fish stock

juice of 1 lime

1–2 tbsp Thai fish sauce

125g (4oz) mangetouts

3 tbsp fresh coriander, roughly torn

salt and ground black pepper

1 Heat the oil in a wok or large non-stick frying pan. Add the curry paste and cook for 1–2 minutes.

2 Add the monkfish and prawns and stir well to coat in the curry paste. Add the coconut milk, stock, lime juice and fish sauce. Stir all the ingredients together and bring just to the boil.

3 Add the mangetouts and simmer for 5 minutes or until the mangetouts and fish are tender. Stir in the coriander and check the seasoning, adding salt and pepper to taste. Serve immediately.

EASY		NUTRITIONAL INFORMATION		Serves
Preparation Time 15 minutes	**Cooking Time** 8–10 minutes	**Per Serving** 252 calories, 8g fat (of which 1g saturates), 9g carbohydrate, 2.2g salt	Gluten free • Dairy free	**4**

Thai Green Shellfish Curry

1 tbsp vegetable oil

1 lemongrass stalk, chopped

2 small red chillies, chopped (see page 36)

a handful of coriander leaves, chopped, plus extra to serve

2 kaffir lime leaves, chopped

1–2 tbsp Thai green curry paste

400ml can coconut milk

450ml (³/₄ pint) vegetable stock

375g (13oz) queen scallops with corals

250g (9oz) raw tiger prawns, peeled and deveined, with tails intact

salt and ground black pepper

jasmine rice to serve

1 Heat the oil in a wok or large frying pan. Add the lemongrass, chillies, coriander and lime leaves and stir-fry for 30 seconds. Add the curry paste and fry for 1 minute.

2 Add the coconut milk and stock and bring to the boil. Simmer for 5–10 minutes until slightly reduced. Season well with salt and pepper.

3 Add the scallops and tiger prawns, bring to the boil and simmer gently for 2–3 minutes until cooked. Divide the jasmine rice among six serving bowls and spoon the curry over the top. Sprinkle with coriander and serve immediately, with rice.

Try Something Different

Use cleaned squid or mussels (see pages 24–25) instead of scallops and prawns.

EASY		NUTRITIONAL INFORMATION		Serves
Preparation Time 10 minutes	**Cooking Time** 10–15 minutes	**Per Serving** 156 calories, 5g fat (of which 1g saturates), 6g carbohydrate, 0.8g salt	Gluten free • Dairy free	**6**

Stir-fried Salmon and Broccoli

2 tsp sesame oil

1 red pepper, seeded and thinly sliced

½ red chilli, thinly sliced (see page 36)

1 garlic clove, crushed

125g (4oz) broccoli florets

2 spring onions, sliced

2 salmon fillets, about 125g (4oz) each, cut into strips

1 tsp Thai fish sauce

2 tsp soy sauce

wholewheat noodles to serve

1 Heat the oil in a wok or large frying pan and add the red pepper, chilli, garlic, broccoli florets and spring onions. Stir-fry over a high heat for 3–4 minutes.

2 Add the salmon, fish sauce and soy sauce and cook for 2 minutes, stirring gently. Serve immediately with wholewheat noodles.

Serves 2	EASY		NUTRITIONAL INFORMATION	
	Preparation Time 10 minutes	**Cooking Time** 5–6 minutes	**Per Serving** 90 calories, 4.1g fat (of which 1g saturates), 9g carbohydrate, 2.7g salt	Dairy free

Cook's Tip

To make spring onion curls, trim spring onions into 7.5cm (3in) lengths, shred finely, then place in a bowl of water with ice cubes for 30 minutes.

Steamed Sesame Salmon

groundnut or vegetable oil to brush

8–12 large Chinese leaves or lettuce leaves

4 salmon steaks, about 150g (5oz) each

½ tsp sesame oil

2 tbsp dry sherry

2 tbsp light soy sauce, plus extra to serve

3 tsp sesame seeds, lightly toasted in a dry wok or heavy-based pan

4 spring onions, shredded, plus extra spring onion curls to garnish

ground white pepper

1 Steam the Chinese leaves or lettuce leaves for 1–2 minutes until soft and pliable. Discard about 2.5cm (1in) of the firm stalk end from each leaf to neaten, and place 2–3 leaves together, slightly overlapping. Put the salmon steaks on top.

2 Mix the sesame oil with the sherry and soy sauce and drizzle the mixture over the salmon. Sprinkle with the shredded spring onions, 2 tsp sesame seeds and pepper to taste.

3 Fold the leaves over the salmon to form neat parcels. Steam for 5–7 minutes or until the fish is cooked and flakes easily.

4 Serve the salmon parcels with the juices spooned over. Sprinkle with the remaining sesame seeds and a little extra soy sauce, garnish with spring onion curls.

EASY		NUTRITIONAL INFORMATION		Serves
Preparation Time 20 minutes	**Cooking Time** 15–18 minutes	**Per Serving** 312 calories, 19g fat (of which 3g saturates), 2g carbohydrate, 1.5g salt	Dairy free	**4**

Teriyaki Salmon with Spinach

550g (1¼ lb) salmon fillet, cut into 1cm (½in) slices

3 tbsp teriyaki sauce

3 tbsp tamari or light soy sauce

2 tbsp vegetable oil

1 tbsp sesame oil

1 tbsp chopped fresh chives

2 tsp grated fresh root ginger

2 garlic cloves, crushed

350g (12oz) soba noodles

350g (12oz) baby spinach leaves

furikake seasoning

1 Gently mix the salmon slices with the teriyaki sauce, then cover, chill and leave to marinate for 1 hour.

2 Mix together the soy sauce, 1 tbsp vegetable oil, sesame oil, chives, ginger and garlic. Set aside.

3 Cook the noodles according to the packet instructions. Drain and put to one side.

4 Heat the remaining vegetable oil in a wok or large frying pan. Remove the salmon from the marinade and add it to the pan. Cook over a high heat until it turns opaque – about 30 seconds. Remove from the pan and put to one side.

5 Add the drained noodles to the pan and stir until warmed through. Stir in the spinach and cook for 1–2 minutes until wilted. Add the soy sauce mixture and stir to combine.

6 Divide the noodles among four deep bowls, then top with the salmon. Sprinkle with furikake seasoning and serve.

Cook's Tip

Furikake seasoning is a Japanese condiment consisting of sesame seeds and chopped seaweed which can be found in major supermarkets and Asian food shops.

Soba noodles are made from buckwheat and are gluten-free. If you have a wheat allergy or gluten intolerance, look for 100% soba on the pack.

Serves 4	EASY		NUTRITIONAL INFORMATION	
	Preparation Time 10 minutes, plus 1 hour marinating	**Cooking Time** 6 minutes	**Per Serving** 672 calories, 30g fat (of which 4g saturates), 66g carbohydrate, 2.9g salt	Dairy free

2

Chicken and Poultry

Try Something Different

Other vegetables are just as good in this dish: try pak choi, button mushrooms, carrots cut into matchsticks, or baby sweetcorn.

Quick Chicken Stir-fry

1 tsp groundnut oil
300g (11oz) skinless chicken breast fillets, sliced
4 spring onions, chopped
200g (7oz) medium rice noodles
100g (3½oz) mangetouts
200g (7oz) purple sprouting broccoli, chopped
2–3 tbsp sweet chilli sauce
freshly chopped coriander and lime wedges (optional) to garnish

1 Heat the oil in a wok or large frying pan and add the chicken and spring onions. Stir-fry over a high heat for 5–6 minutes until the chicken is golden.

2 Meanwhile, soak the rice noodles in boiling water for 4 minutes or according to the packet instructions.

3 Add the mangetouts, broccoli and chilli sauce to the chicken. Continue to stir-fry for 4 minutes.

4 Drain the noodles and add them to the pan. Toss everything together. Scatter the chopped coriander over the top and serve with lime wedges to squeeze over, if you like.

Serves 4	EASY		NUTRITIONAL INFORMATION	
	Preparation Time 10 minutes	**Cooking Time** 12 minutes	**Per Serving** 316 calories, 3g fat (of which 1g saturates), 46g carbohydrate, 0.5g salt	Gluten free • Dairy free

Try Something Different

Replace the chicken with pork escalopes or rump steak, cut into thin strips.

4 skinless chicken breast fillets, cut into strips

1 tbsp ground coriander

2 garlic cloves, finely chopped

4 tbsp vegetable oil

2 tbsp clear honey

Thai fragrant rice to serve

fresh coriander sprigs to garnish

For the peanut sauce

1 tbsp vegetable oil

2 tbsp curry paste

2 tbsp brown sugar

2 tbsp peanut butter

200ml (7fl oz) coconut milk

Chicken with Peanut Sauce

1 Mix the chicken with the ground coriander, garlic, oil and honey. Cover, chill and leave to marinate for 15 minutes.

2 To make the peanut sauce, heat the oil in a pan, add the curry paste, brown sugar and peanut butter and fry for 1 minute. Add the coconut milk and bring to the boil, stirring all the time, then simmer for 5 minutes.

3 Meanwhile, heat a wok or large frying pan and, when hot, stir-fry the chicken and its marinade in batches for 3–4 minutes or until cooked, adding more oil if needed.

4 Serve the chicken on a bed of Thai fragrant rice, with the peanut sauce poured over. Garnish with coriander sprigs.

EASY		NUTRITIONAL INFORMATION		Serves
Preparation Time 10 minutes, plus 15 minutes marinating	**Cooking Time** about 10 minutes	**Per Serving** 408 calories, 20g fat (of which 3g saturates), 19g carbohydrate, 0.5g salt	Gluten free • Dairy free	**4**

Chicken with Vegetables and Noodles

225g (8oz) fine egg noodles

about 2 tbsp vegetable oil

1 skinless chicken breast fillet, cut into very thin strips

2.5cm (1in) piece fresh root ginger, peeled and finely chopped

1 garlic clove, finely chopped

1 red pepper, seeded and thinly sliced

4 spring onions, thinly sliced, plus extra to garnish

2 carrots, thinly sliced

125g (4oz) shiitake or button mushrooms, halved

a handful of bean sprouts (optional)

3 tbsp hoisin sauce

2 tbsp light soy sauce

1 tbsp chilli sauce

sesame seeds to garnish

1 Bring a large pan of water to the boil and cook the noodles for about 3 minutes or according to the packet instructions. Drain thoroughly and toss with a little of the oil to prevent them sticking together; set aside.

2 Heat the remaining oil in a wok or large frying pan. Add the chicken, ginger and garlic and cook over a very high heat until the chicken is browned on the outside and cooked right through, about 5 minutes.

3 Add all the vegetables to the pan and stir-fry over a high heat for about 2 minutes or until they are just cooked, but still crunchy.

4 Stir in the hoisin sauce, soy sauce and chilli sauce and mix well. Add the noodles, toss well to mix and cook for a couple of minutes until heated through. Serve immediately, sprinkled with shredded spring onion and sesame seeds.

Try Something Different

Replace the chicken with thinly sliced turkey escalopes.
Increase the heat of the dish by frying a chopped chilli with the garlic and ginger.

EASY		NUTRITIONAL INFORMATION		Serves
Preparation Time 10 minutes	**Cooking Time** about 12 minutes	**Per Serving** 584 calories, 19g fat (of which 3g saturates), 67g carbohydrate, 4.1g salt	Dairy free	**2**

Try Something Different

Instead of chicken, try this with thinly sliced pork tenderloin.

Chicken with Oyster Sauce

6 tbsp vegetable oil

450g (1lb) skinless chicken breast fillets, cut into bite-size pieces

3 tbsp oyster sauce

1 tbsp dark soy sauce

100ml (3½fl oz) chicken stock

2 tsp lemon juice

1 garlic clove, thinly sliced

6–8 large flat mushrooms, about 250g (9oz) total weight, sliced

125g (4oz) mangetouts

1 tsp cornflour mixed with 1 tbsp water

1 tbsp sesame oil

salt and ground black pepper

1 Heat 3 tbsp oil in a wok or large frying pan. Add the chicken and cook over a high heat, stirring continuously for 2–3 minutes until lightly browned. Remove the chicken with a slotted spoon and drain on kitchen paper.

2 In a bowl, mix the oyster sauce with the soy sauce, chicken stock and lemon juice. Add the chicken and mix thoroughly.

3 Heat the remaining vegetable oil in the pan over a high heat and stir-fry the garlic for about 30 seconds; add the mushrooms and cook for 1 minute. Add the chicken mixture, cover and simmer for 8 minutes.

4 Stir in the mangetouts and cook for a further 2–3 minutes. Remove the pan from the heat and stir in the cornflour mixture. Return the pan to the heat, add the sesame oil and stir until the sauce has thickened. Season with salt and pepper and serve immediately.

Serves	EASY		NUTRITIONAL INFORMATION	
4	**Preparation Time** 10 minutes	**Cooking Time** about 18 minutes	**Per Serving** 330 calories, 21g fat (of which 2.7g saturates), 6g carbohydrate, 1.3g salt	Dairy free

Chicken and Coconut Curry

2 garlic cloves, peeled

1 onion, quartered

1 lemongrass stalk, halved

2.5cm (1in) piece fresh root ginger, peeled and halved

2 small hot chillies (see page 36)

a small handful of fresh coriander

1 tsp ground coriander

grated zest and juice of 1 lime

2 tbsp vegetable oil

6 skinless chicken breast fillets, each cut into three pieces

2 large tomatoes, skinned and chopped

2 tbsp Thai fish sauce

900ml (1½ pints) coconut milk

salt and ground black pepper

basmati rice to serve

finely sliced red chilli to garnish

1 Put the garlic, onion, lemongrass, ginger, chillies, fresh coriander, ground coriander and lime zest and juice in a food processor and whiz to a paste. Add a little water if the mixture gets stuck under the blades.

2 Heat the oil in a wok or large frying pan, add the spice paste and cook over a fairly high heat for 3–4 minutes, stirring constantly. Add the chicken and cook for 5 minutes, stirring to coat in the spice mixture.

3 Add the tomatoes, fish sauce and coconut milk. Simmer, covered, for about 25 minutes or until the chicken is cooked. Season with salt and pepper and serve with basmati rice; garnish with red chilli.

EASY		NUTRITIONAL INFORMATION		Serves
Preparation Time 15 minutes	**Cooking Time** 35 minutes	**Per Serving** 204 calories, 6g fat (of which 1g saturates), 10g carbohydrate, 1.5g salt	Gluten free • Dairy free	**6**

Thai Chicken and Noodle Soup

225g (8oz) firm tofu

vegetable oil for shallow or deep-frying

2.5cm (1in) piece fresh root ginger, peeled and finely chopped

2.5cm (1in) piece fresh or dried galangal, peeled and thinly sliced (optional, see Cook's Tip)

1–2 garlic cloves, crushed

2 lemongrass stalks, halved lengthways and bruised

1 tsp chilli powder

½ tsp ground turmeric

275g (10oz) cooked chicken, skinned and cut into bite-size pieces

175g (6oz) cauliflower, broken into small florets and any thick stems thinly sliced

1 large carrot, cut into matchsticks

600ml (1 pint) coconut milk

600ml (1 pint) chicken or vegetable stock, or water

a few green beans, trimmed and halved

125g (4oz) fine or medium egg noodles

125g (4oz) peeled prawns (optional)

3 spring onions, thinly sliced

75g (3oz) bean sprouts

2 tbsp soy sauce

1 Pat the tofu dry with kitchen paper, then cut it into small cubes, about 1cm (½in) square. Heat the oil in a wok or deep-fryer to 180°C (test by frying a small cube of bread; it should brown in 30 seconds). Fry the tofu, in batches, until golden brown on all sides, about 1 minute. Drain on kitchen paper.

2 Heat 2 tbsp oil in a large pan. Add the ginger, galangal, if using, garlic, lemongrass, chilli powder, turmeric and chicken and cook for 2 minutes, stirring all the time.

3 Add the cauliflower, carrot, coconut milk and stock and bring to the boil, stirring all the time. Reduce the heat and simmer for 10 minutes. Add the beans and simmer for 5 minutes.

4 Meanwhile, bring a large pan of water to the boil and cook the noodles for about 4 minutes or according to the packet instructions.

5 Drain the noodles and add them to the soup with the prawns, if using, tofu, spring onions, bean sprouts and soy sauce. Simmer gently for 5 minutes or until heated through. Serve immediately.

Cook's Tip

Dried galangal, similar in flavour to root ginger, needs to be soaked for 30 minutes before using. It's used chopped or grated in many Thai, Indonesian and Malay dishes.

Serves 4	A LITTLE EFFORT		NUTRITIONAL INFORMATION	
	Preparation Time 20 minutes	**Cooking Time** about 30 minutes	**Per Serving** 384 calories, 15g fat (of which 3g saturates), 36g carbohydrate, 2g salt	Dairy free

Cook's Tip

This is a great way to use leftover turkey.

Thai Red Turkey Curry

3 tbsp vegetable oil

450g (1lb) onions, finely chopped

200g (7oz) green beans, trimmed

125g (4oz) baby sweetcorn, cut on the diagonal

2 red peppers, seeded and cut into thick strips

1 tbsp Thai red curry paste, or to taste

1 red chilli, seeded and finely chopped (see page 36)

1 lemongrass stalk, very finely chopped

4 kaffir lime leaves, bruised

2 tbsp fresh root ginger, peeled and finely chopped

1 garlic clove, crushed

400ml can coconut milk

600ml (1 pint) chicken or turkey stock

450g (1lb) cooked turkey, cut into strips

150g (5oz) bean sprouts

fresh basil leaves to garnish

1 Heat the oil in a wok or large frying pan, add the onions and cook for 4–5 minutes or until soft.

2 Add the beans, baby corn and peppers to the pan and stir-fry for 3–4 minutes. Add the curry paste, chilli, lemongrass, kaffir lime leaves, ginger and garlic and cook for a further 2 minutes, stirring. Remove from the pan and set aside.

3 Add the coconut milk and stock to the pan, bring to the boil and bubble vigorously for 5–10 minutes until reduced by one-quarter. Return the vegetables to the pan with the turkey and bean sprouts. Bring to the boil and simmer for 1–2 minutes until heated through. Serve immediately, garnished with basil leaves.

Serves 6	EASY		NUTRITIONAL INFORMATION	
	Preparation Time 20 minutes	**Cooking Time** 18–25 minutes	**Per Serving** 248 calories, 8g fat (of which 1g saturates), 16g carbohydrate, 1.2g salt	Gluten free • Dairy free

▼ Turkey and Sesame Stir-fry with Noodles

▶ Aubergine in a Hot Sweet and Sour Sauce
(see page 100)

Turkey and Sesame Stir-fry with Noodles

300g (11oz) turkey breast fillets, cut into thin strips

3 tbsp teriyaki marinade

3 tbsp clear honey

500g (1lb 2oz) medium egg noodles

about 1 tbsp sesame oil, plus extra for the noodles

300g (11oz) ready-prepared mixed stir-fry vegetables, such as carrots, broccoli, red cabbage, mangetouts, bean sprouts and purple spring onions

2 tbsp sesame seeds, lightly toasted in a dry wok or heavy-based pan

1 Put the turkey strips in a large bowl with the teriyaki marinade and honey, and stir to coat. Cover and set aside for 5 minutes.

2 Bring a large pan of water to the boil and cook the noodles for about 4 minutes or according to the packet instructions. Drain well, then toss in a little sesame oil.

3 Heat 1 tbsp of the oil in a wok or large frying pan and add the turkey, reserving the marinade. Stir-fry over a very high heat for 2–3 minutes until cooked through and beginning to brown. Add a drop more oil, if needed, then add the vegetables and reserved marinade. Continue to cook over a high heat, stirring, until the vegetables have started to soften and the sauce is warmed through.

4 Scatter with the sesame seeds and serve immediately with the noodles.

EASY		NUTRITIONAL INFORMATION		Serves
Preparation Time 5 minutes, plus 5 minutes marinating	**Cooking Time** 10 minutes	**Per Serving** 672 calories, 18g fat (of which 4.2g saturates), 97g carbohydrate, 0.7g salt	Dairy free	**4**

► Stir-fried Vegetables with Oyster Sauce
(see page 96)
▼ Sweet and Sour Duck

Sweet and Sour Duck

3 tbsp dark soy sauce

1 tbsp dry sherry

1 tsp sesame oil

225g (8oz) duck breast fillets, thinly sliced

1 tbsp sugar

2 tsp cornflour

3 tbsp distilled malt vinegar

1 tbsp tomato ketchup

4 tbsp vegetable oil

125g (4oz) aubergine, sliced

1 red onion, sliced

1 garlic clove, sliced

125g (4oz) carrot, sliced lengthways into strips

125g (4oz) sugarsnap peas or mangetouts

1 mango, peeled, stoned and thinly sliced

noodles to serve

1 Mix 1 tbsp soy sauce with the sherry and sesame oil. Pour the mixture over the duck, cover and leave to marinate for at least 30 minutes.

2 Mix together the sugar, cornflour, vinegar, ketchup and remaining 2 tbsp soy sauce. Set aside.

3 Heat 2 tbsp of the vegetable oil in a wok or large non-stick frying pan. Drain the duck from the marinade and reserve the marinade. Fry the duck slices over a high heat for 3–4 minutes until golden and the fat is crisp. Remove from the pan and set aside.

4 Add 1 tbsp more oil to the pan and fry the aubergine for about 2 minutes on each side until golden. Add the remaining 1 tbsp oil and fry the onion, garlic and carrot for 2–3 minutes, then add the sugarsnap peas and fry for a further 1–2 minutes. Add the mango to the pan along with the duck, the soy sauce mixture and the reserved marinade. Bring to the boil, stirring gently all the time, and allow to bubble for 2–3 minutes until slightly thickened. Serve immediately, with noodles.

EASY		NUTRITIONAL INFORMATION		Serves
Preparation Time 15 minutes, plus marinating	**Cooking Time** about 15 minutes	**Per Serving** 278 calories, 13g fat (of which 2g saturates), 29g carbohydrate, 1.9g salt	Dairy free	**4**

Try Something Different

Add a drained 225g can of bamboo shoots with the other vegetables in step 2, if you like.

Hot Jungle Curry

1 tbsp vegetable oil

350g (12oz) skinless chicken breast fillets, cut into 5cm (2in) strips

2 tbsp Thai red curry paste

2.5cm (1in) piece fresh root ginger, peeled and thinly sliced

125g (4oz) aubergine, cut into bite-size pieces

125g (4oz) baby sweetcorn, halved lengthways

75g (3oz) green beans, trimmed

75g (3oz) button or brown-cap mushrooms, halved if large

2–3 kaffir lime leaves (optional)

450ml ($^3/_4$ pint) chicken stock

2 tbsp Thai fish sauce

grated zest of $^1/_2$ lime, plus extra to garnish

1 tsp tomato purée

1 tbsp soft brown sugar

1 Heat the oil in a wok or large frying pan. Add the chicken and cook, stirring, for 5 minutes or until the chicken turns golden brown.

2 Add the red curry paste and cook for a further 1 minute. Add the ginger, aubergine, sweetcorn, beans, mushrooms and lime leaves, if using, and stir until coated in the red curry paste. Add all the remaining ingredients and bring to the boil. Simmer gently for 10–12 minutes or until the chicken and vegetables are just tender. Serve immediately, sprinkled with lime zest.

Serves 4	EASY		NUTRITIONAL INFORMATION	
	Preparation Time 10 minutes	**Cooking Time** 18–20 minutes	**Per Serving** 160 calories, 5g fat (of which 1g saturates), 5g carbohydrate, 1.1g salt	Gluten free • Dairy free

Thai Green Curry

2 tsp vegetable oil

1 green chilli, seeded and finely chopped (see page 36)

4cm (1½in) piece fresh root ginger, peeled and finely grated

1 lemongrass stalk, cut into 3 pieces

225g (8oz) brown-cap or oyster mushrooms

1 tbsp Thai green curry paste

300ml (½ pint) coconut milk

150ml (¼ pint) chicken stock

1 tbsp Thai fish sauce

1 tsp light soy sauce

350g (12oz) skinless chicken breast fillets, cut into bite-size pieces

350g (12oz) cooked peeled large prawns

fresh coriander sprigs to garnish

1 Heat the oil in a wok or large frying pan, add the chilli, ginger, lemongrass and mushrooms and stir-fry for about 3 minutes or until the mushrooms begin to turn golden. Add the curry paste and fry for a further 1 minute.

2 Pour in the coconut milk, stock, fish sauce and soy sauce and bring to the boil. Stir in the chicken and simmer for about 8 minutes or until the chicken is cooked. Add the prawns and cook for a further 1 minute. Garnish with coriander sprigs and serve immediately.

EASY		NUTRITIONAL INFORMATION		Serves
Preparation Time 10 minutes	**Cooking Time** 15 minutes	**Per Serving** 132 calories, 2g fat (of which 0g saturates), 4g carbohydrate, 1.4g salt	Dairy free	**6**

Try Something Different

Use pork fillet instead of turkey, cutting the fillet into thin slices.

Turkey and Broccoli Stir-fry

2 tbsp vegetable or sunflower oil
500g (1lb 2oz) turkey fillet, cut into strips
2 garlic cloves, crushed
2.5cm (1in) piece fresh root ginger, peeled and grated
1 broccoli head, cut into florets
8 spring onions, finely chopped
150g (5oz) button mushrooms, halved
100g (3½oz) bean sprouts
3 tbsp oyster sauce
1 tbsp light soy sauce
125ml (4fl oz) hot chicken stock
juice of ½ lemon

1 Heat 1 tbsp of the oil in a wok or large non-stick frying pan, add the turkey strips and stir-fry for 4–5 minutes until golden and cooked through. Remove from the pan and set aside.

2 Heat the remaining oil in the same pan over a medium heat, add the garlic and ginger and cook for 30 seconds, stirring all the time so that they don't burn. Add the broccoli, onions and mushrooms, increase the heat and cook for 2–3 minutes until the vegetables start to brown but are still crisp.

3 Return the turkey to the pan and add the bean sprouts, oyster and soy sauces, stock and lemon juice. Cook for 1–2 minutes, stirring well, until everything is heated through.

Serves 4	EASY		NUTRITIONAL INFORMATION	
	Preparation Time 15 minutes	**Cooking Time** 8–12 minutes	**Per Serving** 254 calories, 8g fat (of which 1g saturates), 8g carbohydrate, 1.3g salt	Dairy free

4 duck breast fillets, about 175g (6oz) each

1½ tbsp clear honey

3 tbsp vegetable oil

1 bunch of spring onions, cut into 2.5cm (1in) lengths

1 large green pepper, seeded and cut into thin strips

225g (8oz) mangetouts

2 garlic cloves, crushed

2–3 good pinches of Chinese five-spice powder

3 tbsp caster sugar

3 tbsp dark soy sauce

3 tbsp wine vinegar

16 water chestnuts, sliced

40g (1½ oz) toasted cashew nuts

salt

Crispy Duck with Mangetouts

1 Preheat the oven to 180°C (160°C fan oven) mark 4. Prick the duck skin all over with a skewer or fork and rub well with salt. Put the breasts, skin side up, on a rack or trivet in a roasting tin and cook in the oven, uncovered, for 15 minutes.

2 Remove the duck breasts from the oven and brush the skins with honey. Return them to the oven and cook for a further 5–10 minutes or until the duck is cooked through. Leave to cool, then cut into strips.

3 Heat the oil in a wok or large frying pan. Add the spring onions, green pepper, mangetouts, garlic and five-spice powder and stir-fry for 2 minutes. Add the sugar, soy sauce, vinegar and duck strips and toss in the sauce to heat through and glaze. Add the water chestnuts and cook until heated through.

4 Serve immediately, sprinkled with toasted cashew nuts.

EASY		NUTRITIONAL INFORMATION		Serves
Preparation Time 15 minutes, plus cooling	**Cooking Time** about 30 minutes	**Per Serving** 308 calories, 17g fat (of which 3g saturates), 18g carbohydrate, 1.7g salt	Dairy free	**6**

Duck with Pineapple

4 duck breast fillets, about 175g (6oz) each

2 tsp clear honey

3 carrots, cut into thin strips

1 bunch of spring onions, sliced diagonally

2.5cm (1in) piece fresh root ginger, peeled and cut into very thin strips

1 garlic clove, crushed

125g (4oz) mangetouts

½ small fresh pineapple, peeled, cored and cut into chunks

3 tbsp dark soy sauce

3 tbsp malt vinegar

3 tbsp caster sugar

1 tbsp cornflour

175ml (6fl oz) fresh orange juice

salt

1 Preheat the oven to 180°C (160°C fan oven) mark 4. Prick the duck skin all over with a skewer or fork and rub well with salt. Put the breasts, skin side up, on a rack or trivet in a roasting tin and cook in the oven, uncovered, for 15 minutes.

2 Remove the duck breasts from the oven and brush the skins with honey. Return them to the oven and cook for a further 5–10 minutes or until golden and cooked through. Transfer the duck breasts to a plate and leave to rest for 5 minutes. Reserve the fat in the roasting tin.

3 To make the sauce, heat 3 tbsp of the reserved duck fat in a wok or large frying pan, add the carrots, spring onions, ginger, garlic and mangetouts and stir-fry for 2 minutes. Using a slotted spoon, remove the vegetables from the pan and set aside.

4 Add the pineapple to the pan and fry gently for about 20 seconds until heated through. Remove from the pan and keep warm.

5 Stir the soy sauce, vinegar and sugar into the pan. Blend the cornflour with the orange juice, add it to the pan and cook for 2 minutes, stirring. Return the vegetables to the pan and cook until heated through.

6 Cut the duck breasts diagonally into fairly thin slices. Arrange the duck and pineapple on hot serving plates and spoon the sauce and vegetables over the top.

Serves 4	EASY		NUTRITIONAL INFORMATION	
	Preparation Time 15 minutes, plus 5 minutes resting	**Cooking Time** about 30 minutes	**Per Serving** 382 calories, 12g fat (of which 2g saturates), 40g carbohydrate, 2.6g salt	Dairy free

3

Pork, Lamb and Beef

Pork and Vegetable Stir-fry

2 tbsp light soy sauce

2 tbsp dry sherry

2 garlic cloves, crushed

5cm (2in) piece fresh root ginger, peeled and grated

1 tsp cornflour

450g (1lb) pork tenderloin, cut into thin slices

1 tbsp groundnut oil

1 large carrot, cut into matchsticks

225g (8oz) broccoli, cut into small florets

8 spring onions, shredded

150g (5oz) bean sprouts

salt and ground black pepper

rice to serve

1 Put 1 tbsp soy sauce, 1tbsp sherry, the garlic, ginger and cornflour in a large bowl and mix well. Add the pork to the soy sauce mixture and stir thoroughly, then set aside to marinate for 15 minutes.

2 Heat a wok or large non-stick frying pan until very hot and add the groundnut oil. Stir-fry the pork slices in two batches, cooking each batch for 2–3 minutes until the meat is browned. Set aside and keep warm.

3 Reheat the pan, then add the carrot and broccoli and stir-fry for 5 minutes. Add the remaining sherry and soy sauce and 4 tbsp cold water and bring just to the boil. Return the pork to the pan and stir-fry for 2–3 minutes until heated through. Add the spring onions and bean sprouts and stir-fry for 1 minute. Season with salt and pepper, then serve with rice.

Serves	EASY		NUTRITIONAL INFORMATION	
4	**Preparation Time** 15 minutes, plus 15 minutes marinating	**Cooking Time** about 15 minutes	**Per Serving** 220 calories, 8g fat (of which 2g saturates), 7g carbohydrate, 1.6g salt	Dairy free

700g (1½lb) belly pork rashers

2 tbsp vegetable oil

1 garlic clove, crushed

1cm (½in) piece fresh root ginger, peeled and finely chopped

1 onion, quartered lengthways, halved crossways and separated into layers

4 spring onions, cut into 2.5cm (1in) pieces

½ red pepper, seeded and cut into 1cm (½in) squares

½ yellow pepper, seeded and cut into 1cm (½in) squares

½ orange pepper, seeded and cut into 1cm (½in) squares

1 tbsp light soy sauce

1 tbsp dry sherry

150g (5oz) black bean sauce

noodles to serve

Twice-cooked Pork with Black Bean Sauce

1 Cook the belly pork rashers in boiling water for 30 minutes. Drain well and leave to cool. Remove the rinds and any bones and cut the rashers into 2.5cm (1in) pieces.

2 Heat the oil in a wok or large frying pan, add the pork and stir-fry for 3–4 minutes until crisp and light golden.

3 Add the garlic, ginger, onion, spring onions and peppers to the pan and stir-fry for 2 minutes. Add the soy sauce, sherry and black bean sauce and stir-fry for 1–2 minutes until heated through. Serve immediately, with noodles.

EASY		NUTRITIONAL INFORMATION		Serves
Preparation Time 12 minutes	**Cooking Time** about 40 minutes	**Per Serving** 600 calories, 47g fat (of which 15g saturates), 13g carbohydrate, 6.6g salt	Dairy free	**4**

Stir-fried Pork with Chinese Greens

200g (7oz) pork tenderloin or fillet, cut into strips

2 tbsp finely chopped fresh root ginger

3 tbsp soy sauce

2 garlic cloves, crushed

700g (1½lb) mixed vegetables, such as pak choi, broccoli, carrots, bean sprouts and sugarsnap peas

3 tbsp vegetable oil

5 spring onions, cut into four lengthways

1 red chilli, seeded and sliced (see page 36)

1 tbsp sesame oil

2 tbsp dry sherry

2 tbsp oyster sauce

salt and ground black pepper

1 Put the pork in a non-metallic dish with the ginger, 2 tbsp soy sauce and the garlic. Set aside to marinate for at least 30 minutes.

2 Meanwhile, prepare the vegetables. Cut the pak choi into quarters, separate the broccoli into florets and cut the carrot into ribbons, using a vegetable peeler.

3 Heat a wok or large frying pan over a high heat and add the oil. Stir-fry the pork in two batches, cooking each batch for 2–3 minutes until the meat is browned. Season the pork with salt and pepper, set aside and keep warm.

4 Add the spring onions and chilli to the pan and cook for 30 seconds. Add all the vegetables and stir-fry for 4–5 minutes. Return the pork to the pan. Add the remaining soy sauce, sesame oil, sherry and oyster sauce, then stir-fry for 2 minutes or until the sauce is syrupy. Serve immediately.

Get Ahead

To prepare ahead Complete to the end of step 3, then cool, wrap and chill the pork and vegetables separately for up to four hours.
To use Complete the recipe until the pork is piping hot.

EASY		NUTRITIONAL INFORMATION		Serves
Preparation Time 15 minutes, plus 30 minutes marinating	**Cooking Time** about 15 minutes	**Per Serving** 234 calories, 15g fat (of which 2g saturates), 6g carbohydrate, 1.8g salt	Dairy free	**4**

▶ Asparagus with Crab and Pineapple (see page 36)
▶ Five-minute Stir-fry (see page 32)
▼ Pork Stir-fry with Chilli and Mango

Pork Stir-fry with Chilli and Mango

75g (3oz) medium egg noodles

1 tsp groundnut oil

½ red chilli, seeded and finely chopped (see page 36)

125g (4oz) pork stir-fry strips

1 head pak choi, roughly chopped

1 tbsp soy sauce

½ ripe mango, sliced

1 Bring a large pan of water to the boil and cook the noodles for about 4 minutes or according to the packet instructions. Drain, then plunge into cold water. Set aside.

2 Meanwhile, heat the oil in a wok or large frying pan until very hot. Add the chilli and pork and stir-fry for 3–4 minutes. Add the pak choi and soy sauce and cook for a further 2–3 minutes. Add the mango and toss to combine.

3 Drain the noodles and add them to the pan. Toss well and cook for 1–2 minutes until heated through. Serve immediately.

Serves 4	EASY		NUTRITIONAL INFORMATION	
	Preparation Time 5 minutes	**Cooking Time** about 10 minutes	**Per Serving** 390 calories, 11g fat (of which 4g saturates), 44g carbohydrate, 1g salt	Dairy free

700g (1½lb) boned belly pork, rind removed

175g (6oz) each pak choi and carrots

2 tbsp groundnut oil

125g (4oz) each red onions, thinly and mangetouts

1 red pepper, seeded and very thinly sliced

2 tbsp light soy sauce

For the marinade

2.5cm (1in) piece fresh root ginger, peeled and finely grated

3 tbsp tomato ketchup

2 tbsp each lemon juice and oil

1 tbsp each paprika and clear honey

Stir-fried Sweet Pork

1 Cut the pork into thin slices about 5mm (¼ in) thick and 5cm (2in) wide. Put them in a pan, cover with cold water, bring slowly to the boil and simmer for 10 minutes. Drain well.

2 Meanwhile, put all the marinade ingredients in a small bowl and mix well. Add the warm, drained pork to the bowl and stir well to coat. Cover and marinate for at least 15 minutes.

3 Cut the white part of the pak choi into thick slices, then slice the green leaves. Keep them separate. Cut the carrots into matchsticks. Slice the red onions thinly and halve the mangetouts diagonally.

4 Drain the pork and reserve the marinade. Heat 1 tbsp oil in a wok or large frying pan. Fry the pork over a high heat, in two batches, for 3–4 minutes until crisp and light golden. Remove from the pan and set aside.

5 Wipe the pan with kitchen paper to remove any residue, then heat the remaining 1 tbsp oil in the pan and stir-fry the onions for 4–5 minutes until they begin to soften. Add the carrots and stir-fry for 3–4 minutes. Add the red pepper and white part of the pak choi and fry for 2–3 minutes. Add the mangetouts and stir-fry for a further 1 minute.

6 Return the pork to the pan with any reserved marinade and the soy sauce. Cook for 1–2 minutes until heated through. At the last minute, stir through the pak choi leaves until wilted and serve immediately.

Cook's Tips

If you cannot find pak choi, use Chinese leaves.
If you want the pork to have a more intense flavour, leave it to marinate for 30 minutes or longer.

EASY		NUTRITIONAL INFORMATION		Serves
Preparation Time 30 minutes, plus at least 15 minutes marinating	**Cooking Time** 30–35 minutes	**Per Serving** 609 calories, 48g fat (of which 15g saturates), 14g carbohydrate, 7.2g salt	Dairy free	**4**

Cook's Tip

Creamed coconut is a solid white block of coconut which can be added directly in chunks to sauces or reconstituted with water.

Stir-fried Pork with Egg Noodles

150g (5oz) medium egg noodles

450g (1lb) pork escalope, cut into thin strips

2 tsp soy sauce

4–6 tbsp sunflower oil

125g (4oz) carrots, cut into matchsticks

225g (8oz) broccoli, cut into florets

150g (5oz) sugarsnap peas, halved diagonally

125g (4oz) mushrooms, thickly sliced

1 bunch of spring onions, thinly sliced

3 tbsp Thai green curry paste

150g (5oz) creamed coconut, roughly chopped and melted in 300ml (½ pint) boiling water (see Cook's Tip)

150ml (¼ pint) chicken stock

Thai fish sauce (optional)

salt and ground black pepper

1 Bring a pan of water to the boil and cook the noodles for 4 minutes or according to the packet instructions. Drain, then plunge into cold water. Set aside.

2 Season the pork with salt, pepper and soy sauce. Heat 1 tbsp oil in a wok or large frying pan. Fry the pork in two batches over a high heat, cooking each batch for 2–3 minutes until lightly browned, adding extra oil if necessary. Remove and set aside.

3 Heat 3 tbsp oil and stir-fry the carrots, broccoli and sugarsnap peas for 2–3 minutes. Add the mushrooms and spring onions, reserving a few to garnish, and fry for 1–2 minutes. Remove and set aside.

4 Add the curry paste, coconut and chicken stock to the pan. Bring to the boil and simmer for 5 minutes. Drain the noodles and add to the pan with the pork and vegetables. Stir well, bring to the boil and simmer for 1–2 minutes to heat through. Season with salt and pepper and a splash of fish sauce, if you like. Serve immediately, garnished with spring onions.

Serves	EASY		NUTRITIONAL INFORMATION	
4	**Preparation Time** 15 minutes	**Cooking Time** about 20 minutes	**Per Serving** 778 calories, 55g fat (of which 27g saturates), 37g carbohydrate, 1g salt	Dairy free

▷ Prawns with Okra (see page 42)
▽ Lamb and Bamboo Shoot Red Curry
▷ Pork and Vegetable Stir-fry (see page 72)

2 tbsp sunflower oil

1 large onion, cut into wedges

2 garlic cloves, finely chopped

450g (1lb) lean boneless lamb, cut into 3cm (1¼ in) cubes

2 tbsp Thai red curry paste

150ml (¼ pint) lamb or beef stock

2 tbsp Thai fish sauce

2 tsp soft brown sugar

200g can bamboo shoots, drained and thinly sliced

1 red pepper, seeded and thinly sliced

2 tbsp freshly chopped mint

1 tbsp freshly chopped basil

25g (1oz) unsalted peanuts, toasted

rice to serve

Lamb and Bamboo Shoot Red Curry

1 Heat the oil in a wok or large frying pan, add the onion and garlic and fry over a medium heat for 5 minutes.

2 Add the lamb and the curry paste and stir-fry for 5 minutes. Add the stock, fish sauce and sugar. Bring to the boil, then lower the heat, cover and simmer gently for 20 minutes.

3 Stir the bamboo shoots, red pepper and herbs into the curry and cook, uncovered, for a further 10 minutes. Stir in the peanuts and serve immediately, with rice.

EASY		NUTRITIONAL INFORMATION		Serves
Preparation Time 10 minutes	**Cooking Time** 45 minutes	**Per Serving** 397 calories, 25g fat (of which 8g saturates), 17g carbohydrate, 0.4g salt	Gluten free • Dairy free	**4**

▶ Chicken with Vegetables and Noodles
  (see page 55)
▼ Szechuan Beef
▶ Asparagus and Mangetouts with Lemon
  Sauce (see page 95)

350g (12oz) beef skirt or rump steak, cut into thin strips

5 tbsp hoisin sauce

4 tbsp dry sherry

2 tbsp vegetable oil

2 red or green chillies, finely chopped (see page 36)

1 large onion, thinly sliced

2 garlic cloves, crushed

2 red peppers, seeded and cut into diamond shapes

2.5cm (1in) piece fresh root ginger, peeled and grated

225g can bamboo shoots, drained and sliced

1 tbsp sesame oil

Szechuan Beef

1 Put the beef in a bowl, add the hoisin sauce and
   sherry and stir to coat. Cover and leave to marinate
   for 30 minutes.

2 Heat the vegetable oil in a wok or large frying pan
   until smoking hot. Add the chillies, onion and garlic
   and stir-fry over a medium heat for 3–4 minutes
   until softened. Remove with a slotted spoon and set
   aside. Add the red peppers, increase the heat and
   stir-fry for a few seconds. Remove and set aside.

3 Add the steak and marinade to the pan in batches.
   Stir-fry each batch over a high heat for about
   1 minute, removing with a slotted spoon.

4 Return the vegetables to the pan. Add the ginger
   and bamboo shoots, then the beef, and stir-fry for a
   further 1 minute until heated through. Transfer to a
   warmed serving dish, sprinkle the sesame oil over the
   top and serve immediately.

Serves	EASY		NUTRITIONAL INFORMATION	
4	**Preparation Time** 15 minutes, plus marinating	**Cooking Time** 5–10 minutes	**Per Serving** 298 calories, 14g fat (of which 4g saturates), 15g carbohydrate, 0.6g salt	Dairy free

Beef with Mushrooms and Oyster Sauce

175–225g (6–8oz) rump steak, cut into thin strips

2 tbsp oyster sauce

2 tbsp dry sherry

25g (1oz) dried black or shiitake mushrooms soaked in boiling water for 30 minutes

2 tbsp vegetable oil

1 small onion, thinly sliced

1 garlic clove, crushed

2.5cm (1in) piece fresh root ginger, peeled and cut into thin strips

2 carrots, cut into matchsticks

2 tsp cornflour

salt and ground black pepper

1 Put the steak, oyster sauce and sherry in a bowl and add salt and pepper to taste. Stir well to mix, then cover and marinate in the refrigerator for 30 minutes. Drain the mushrooms and reserve the soaking liquid. Squeeze the mushrooms dry; discard any hard stalks.

2 Heat the oil in a wok or large frying pan. Add the onion and garlic and stir-fry gently for about 5 minutes until soft but not coloured.

3 Add the mushrooms, ginger and carrots to the pan and stir-fry over medium heat for about 6 minutes until slightly softened. Remove the vegetables with a slotted spoon and set aside.

4 Add the beef and marinade to the pan and stir-fry for 2–3 minutes, until the beef is tender. Mix the cornflour with 4 tbsp of the soaking water from the mushrooms. Pour the mixture into the pan, put the vegetables back in and stir-fry until the sauce is thickened. Taste and adjust the seasoning with salt and pepper, if necessary. Serve immediately.

EASY		NUTRITIONAL INFORMATION		Serves
Preparation Time 15 minutes, plus soaking and marinating	**Cooking Time** about 15 minutes	**Per Serving** 390 calories, 22g fat (of which 6g saturates), 19g carbohydrate, 0.9g salt	Dairy free	**2**

Thai Beef Curry

4 cloves

1 tsp coriander seeds

1 tsp cumin seeds

seeds from 3 cardamom pods

2 garlic cloves, roughly chopped

2.5cm (1in) piece fresh root ginger, peeled and roughly chopped

1 small onion, roughly chopped

2 tbsp sunflower oil

1 tbsp sesame oil

1 tbsp Thai red curry paste

1 tsp turmeric

450g (1lb) sirloin steak, cut into 3cm (1¼in) cubes

225g (8oz) potatoes, quartered

4 tomatoes, quartered

1 tsp sugar

1 tbsp light soy sauce

300ml (½ pint) coconut milk

150ml (¼ pint) beef stock

4 small red chillies, bruised (see page 36)

50g (2oz) cashew nuts

rice and stir-fried green vegetables to serve

1 Put the cloves, coriander, cumin and cardamom seeds in a small heavy-based frying pan and fry over a high heat for 1–2 minutes until the spices release their aroma. Be careful that they do not burn. Leave to cool slightly, then grind to a powder in a spice grinder or blender.

2 Put the garlic, ginger and onion in a blender or food processor and whiz to form a smooth paste. Heat the sunflower and sesame oils in a wok or deep frying pan. Add the onion purée and the curry paste and stir-fry for 5 minutes, then add the ground roasted spices and turmeric and fry for a further 5 minutes.

3 Add the beef to the pan and fry for 5 minutes until browned on all sides. Add the potatoes, tomatoes, sugar, soy sauce, coconut milk, stock and chillies to the pan. Bring to the boil, then lower the heat, cover and simmer gently for about 15 minutes or until the beef is tender and the potatoes are cooked.

4 Stir in the cashew nuts and serve the curry with rice and stir-fried vegetables.

Serves	A LITTLE EFFORT		NUTRITIONAL INFORMATION	
4	**Preparation Time** 20 minutes, plus cooling	**Cooking Time** about 30 minutes	**Per Serving** 443 calories, 26g fat (of which 7g saturates), 23g carbohydrate, 1.2g salt	Dairy free

Marinated Beef and Vegetable Stir-fry

2 rump steaks, about 175g (6oz) each, trimmed

1 tsp vegetable oil

300g pack straight-to-wok noodles

1 red pepper, seeded and thinly sliced

300g (11oz) cabbage, shredded

2 carrots, cut into matchsticks

150g (5oz) shiitake mushrooms, sliced

300g (11oz) bean sprouts

For the sauce

1 red chilli, finely chopped (see page 36)

1 garlic clove, finely chopped

2 tbsp soy sauce

2 tbsp sweet chilli sauce

juice of 1 lime

1 First, make the sauce. Put all the sauce ingredients in a large shallow bowl and mix well. Add the steaks and turn to coat. Cover and chill in the refrigerator for up to 24 hours, if you like.

2 Heat the oil in a wok or large frying pan over a high heat. Remove the steaks from the sauce, reserving the sauce, and cook them for 1–2 minutes on each side. Remove from the pan and set aside.

3 Add the noodles, red pepper, cabbage, carrots and mushrooms to the pan and stir-fry over a high heat for 2–3 minutes. Add the bean sprouts and the reserved sauce and stir-fry for a further 2–3 minutes.

4 Thinly slice the steak and add it to the pan. Toss everything together and serve immediately.

Serves 4	EASY		NUTRITIONAL INFORMATION	
	Preparation Time 15 minutes, plus up to 24 hours chilling	**Cooking Time** about 10 minutes	**Per Serving** 543 calories, 15g fat (of which 4g saturates), 74g carbohydrate, 1.8g salt	Dairy free

Cook's Tip

Wasabi paste is a Japanese condiment, green in colour and extremely hot – a little goes a long way. It is available from some supermarkets.

Tamari is a type of Japanese soy sauce; it is not made with wheat and is gluten-free.

Teriyaki Beef Stir-fry

450g (1lb) beef fillet, sliced as thinly as possible, then cut into 1cm (½in) wide strips

2 tbsp vegetable or groundnut oil

225g (8oz) carrots, cut into matchsticks

½ cucumber, seeded and cut into matchsticks

4–6 spring onions, thinly sliced diagonally

noodles tossed in a little sesame oil and wasabi paste (optional, see Cook's Tip) to serve

For the teriyaki marinade

4 tbsp tamari (see Cook's Tip)

4 tbsp mirin or medium sherry

1 garlic clove, finely chopped

2.5cm (1in) piece fresh root ginger, peeled and finely chopped

1 First, make the marinade. Put all the ingredients for the marinade in a shallow bowl and mix well. Add the beef and turn to coat. Cover and marinate in the refrigerator for at least 30 minutes, preferably overnight.

2 Drain the beef, reserving any marinade. Heat a wok or large frying pan, then add the oil and heat until it is smoking. Add the carrots, cucumber and spring onions and fry over a high heat for 2 minutes until the edges are well browned. Remove from the pan and set aside.

3 Add the beef to the pan and stir-fry over a very high heat for 2 minutes.

4 Return the vegetables to the pan and add the reserved marinade. Stir-fry for 1–2 minutes until heated through. Serve immediately with noodles tossed in a little sesame oil and a small amount of wasabi paste if you like.

EASY		NUTRITIONAL INFORMATION		Serves
Preparation Time 20 minutes, plus marinating	**Cooking Time** 5 minutes	**Per Serving** 275 calories, 16g fat (of which 5g saturates), 6g carbohydrate, 2g salt	Gluten free • Dairy free	**4**

1 tsp chilli oil

1 tbsp soy sauce

1 tbsp clear honey

1 garlic clove, crushed

1 large red chilli, seeded and chopped (see page 36)

400g (14oz) lean beef, cut into strips

1 tsp sunflower oil

1 broccoli head, shredded

200g (7oz) mangetouts, halved

1 red pepper, seeded and cut into strips

soba noodles or rice to serve

Sweet Chilli Beef Stir-fry

1 Put the chilli oil, soy sauce, honey, garlic and chilli in a medium shallow bowl and stir well. Add the strips of beef and toss in the marinade.

2 Heat the oil in a wok or large frying pan over a high heat until it is very hot. Fry the strips of beef in two batches, cooking each batch for 2–3 minutes until tender. Remove the beef from the pan and set aside. Wipe the pan with kitchen paper to remove any residue.

3 Add the broccoli, mangetouts, red pepper and 2 tbsp water to the pan. Stir-fry for 5–6 minutes until the vegetables start to soften. Return the beef to the pan and cook until heated through. Serve immediately, with noodles or rice.

Serves 4	EASY		NUTRITIONAL INFORMATION	
	Preparation Time 10 minutes	**Cooking Time** 10–11 minutes	**Per Serving** 271 calories, 12g fat (of which 4g saturates), 10g carbohydrate, 0.9g salt	Dairy free

Try Something Different

Instead of lamb try this with slices of turkey breast.

Sesame Lamb

125g (4oz) fresh white breadcrumbs

50g (2oz) sesame seeds

450g (1lb) lean boneless lamb, cut into 5mm ($^1/_4$ in) thick slices

2 medium eggs, beaten

6 tbsp groundnut or sunflower oil

1 onion, sliced

3 carrots, cut into strips

225g (8oz) broccoli, cut into florets

2.5cm (1in) piece fresh root ginger, peeled and grated

450ml ($^3/_4$ pint) chicken stock

2 tbsp dry sherry

1$^1/_2$ tbsp cornflour

1 tbsp dark soy sauce

salt and ground black pepper

a few drops of sesame oil to serve

1 Mix the breadcrumbs with the sesame seeds and season with salt and pepper. Dip the lamb slices in the beaten egg, then coat them in the breadcrumb mixture, pressing the breadcrumbs on firmly with your fingertips.

2 Heat 2 tbsp oil in a wok or large frying pan, add half the lamb slices and fry for about 2 minutes on each side until golden. Remove from the pan, drain and keep warm. Cook the remaining lamb in the same way, using another 2 tbsp oil.

3 Wipe the pan clean and heat the remaining oil. Add the onion, carrots, broccoli and ginger and stir-fry for 2 minutes. Add the stock and sherry, cover and cook the vegetables for 1 minute.

4 Blend the cornflour and soy sauce with 1 tbsp water. Stir the mixture into the pan and cook for 2 minutes, stirring constantly. Return the lamb slices to the pan and cook for 1–2 minutes until heated through. Sprinkle with sesame oil and serve immediately.

EASY		NUTRITIONAL INFORMATION		Serves
Preparation Time 15 minutes	**Cooking Time** 15 minutes	**Per Serving** 661 calories, 41g fat (of which 10g saturates), 40g carbohydrate, 2.3g salt	Dairy free	**4**

4

Vegetables and Vegetarian Dishes

Summer Vegetable Stir-fry

125g (4oz) baby carrots, scrubbed and trimmed

1 tbsp sesame seeds

2 tbsp sunflower oil

2 garlic cloves, roughly chopped

125g (4oz) baby courgettes, halved lengthways

1 large yellow pepper, seeded and cut into thick strips

125g (4oz) thin asparagus spears, trimmed

125g (4oz) cherry tomatoes, halved

2 tbsp balsamic or sherry vinegar

1 tsp sesame oil

salt and ground black pepper

1 Blanch the baby carrots in boiling salted water for 2 minutes, then drain and pat dry.

2 Toast the sesame seeds in a hot dry wok or large frying pan over a medium heat, stirring until they turn golden. Tip on to a plate.

3 Return the wok or frying pan to the heat, add the sunflower oil and heat until it is smoking. Add the chopped garlic to the oil and stir-fry for 20 seconds. Add the carrots, courgettes, yellow pepper and asparagus. Stir-fry over a high heat for 1 minute.

4 Add the cherry tomatoes and season to taste with salt and pepper. Stir-fry for 3–4 minutes until the vegetables are just tender. Add the balsamic vinegar and sesame oil, toss well and sprinkle with the toasted sesame seeds. Serve immediately.

Try Something Different

Vary the vegetables, but always blanch the harder ones first. For a winter vegetable stir-fry, use cauliflower and broccoli florets, carrot sticks, 2–3 sliced spring onions and a little chopped fresh root ginger.

EASY		NUTRITIONAL INFORMATION		Serves
Preparation Time 15 minutes	**Cooking Time** 7–8 minutes	**Per Serving** 78 calories, 4g fat (of which 1g saturates), 7g carbohydrate, 0g salt	Vegetarian Gluten free • Dairy free	**4**

▶ Sesame and Cabbage Rolls (see page 104)
▼ Sweet Chilli Tofu Stir-fry
▶ Vegetable Fried Rice (see page 113)

Sweet Chilli Tofu Stir-fry

200g (7oz) firm tofu

4 tbsp sweet chilli sauce

2 tbsp light soy sauce

1 tbsp sesame seeds

2 tbsp toasted sesame oil

600g (1lb 5oz) ready-prepared mixed stir-fry vegetables, such as carrots, broccoli, mangetouts and bean sprouts

a handful of pea shoots or young salad leaves to garnish

1 Drain the tofu, pat it dry and cut it into large cubes. Put the tofu in a shallow container and pour over 1 tbsp sweet chilli sauce and 1 tbsp light soy sauce. Cover and marinate for 10 minutes.

2 Meanwhile, toast the sesame seeds in a hot wok or large frying pan until golden. Tip on to a plate.

3 Return the wok or frying pan to the heat and add 1 tbsp sesame oil. Add the marinated tofu and stir-fry for 5 minutes until golden. Remove and set aside.

4 Heat the remaining 1 tbsp oil in the pan, add the vegetables and stir-fry for 3–4 minutes until just tender. Stir in the cooked tofu.

5 Pour the remaining sweet chilli sauce and soy sauce into the pan, toss well and cook for a further 1 minute until heated through. Sprinkle with the toasted sesame seeds and pea shoots or salad leaves and serve immediately.

Serves 4	EASY		NUTRITIONAL INFORMATION	
	Preparation Time 5 minutes, plus 10 minutes marinating	**Cooking Time** 12 minutes	**Per Serving** 167 calories, 11g fat (of which 2g saturates), 5g carbohydrate, 1.6g salt	Vegetarian • Dairy free

Try Something Different

Try other vegetables, such as thinly sliced leeks, spring onions or pak choi.

Stir-fried Green Vegetables

2 tbsp vegetable oil

225g (8oz) courgettes, thinly sliced

175g (6oz) mangetouts

25g (1oz) butter

175g (6oz) frozen peas, thawed

salt and ground black pepper

1 Heat the oil in a wok or large frying pan, add the courgettes and stir-fry for 1–2 minutes. Add the mangetouts and cook for 1 minute. Add the butter and peas and cook for 1 minute. Season to taste with salt and pepper and serve immediately.

EASY		NUTRITIONAL INFORMATION		Serves
Preparation Time 5 minutes	**Cooking Time** 3–4 minutes	**Per Serving** 100 calories, 8g fat (of which 3g saturates), 5g carbohydrate, 0.1g salt	Vegetarian • Gluten free	**6**

Stir-fried Beans with Cherry Tomatoes

350g (12oz) green beans, trimmed

2 tsp olive oil

1 large garlic clove, crushed

150g (5oz) cherry or baby plum tomatoes, halved

2 tbsp freshly chopped flat-leafed parsley

salt and ground black pepper

1 Cook the beans in boiling salted water for 4–5 minutes, then drain well.

2 Heat the oil in a wok or large frying pan over a high heat. Stir-fry the beans with the garlic and tomatoes for 2–3 minutes until the beans are tender and the tomatoes are just beginning to soften without losing their shape. Season well with salt and pepper, stir in the parsley and serve.

Serves 6	EASY		NUTRITIONAL INFORMATION	
	Preparation Time 10 minutes	**Cooking Time** about 8 minutes	**Per Serving** 30 calories, 1.5g fat (of which trace saturates), 3g carbohydrate, 0g salt	Vegetarian Gluten free • Dairy free

Asparagus and Mangetouts with Lemon Sauce

225g (8oz) asparagus spears, trimmed and cut diagonally into three pieces

1 tbsp sesame seeds

1 tbsp vegetable oil

1 tsp sesame oil

225g (8oz) mangetouts

1 garlic clove, crushed

2 tbsp dry sherry

1 tbsp caster sugar

2 tsp light soy sauce

grated zest and juice of 1 lemon

1 tsp cornflour

salt

strips of lemon zest to garnish

1 Cook the asparagus in a pan of boiling salted water for about 5 minutes until just tender. Drain well.

2 Meanwhile, toast the sesame seeds in a hot wok or large frying pan until golden. Tip on to a plate.

3 Return the wok or frying pan to the heat and add the vegetable and sesame oils. Add the mangetouts, garlic and asparagus and stir-fry for 2 minutes.

4 Put the sherry, sugar, soy sauce, lemon zest and juice, cornflour and 5 tbsp water in a bowl and mix well.

5 Pour the mixture into the pan and cook, stirring, until the sauce thickens and coats the vegetables. Sprinkle with the toasted sesame seeds, garnish with lemon zest and serve immediately.

EASY		NUTRITIONAL INFORMATION		Serves
Preparation Time 5–10 minutes	**Cooking Time** 10 minutes	**Per Serving** 114 calories, 6g fat (of which 1g saturates), 10g carbohydrate, 0g salt	Vegetarian • Dairy free	**4**

Stir-fried Vegetables with Oyster Sauce

175g (6oz) firm tofu
vegetable oil for shallow and deep-frying
2 garlic cloves, thinly sliced
1 green pepper, seeded and sliced
225g (8oz) broccoli, cut into small florets
125g (4oz) green beans, trimmed and halved
50g (2oz) bean sprouts
50g (2oz) canned straw mushrooms, drained
125g (4oz) canned water chestnuts, drained
coriander sprigs to garnish

For the sauce
100ml (3½fl oz) vegetable stock
2 tbsp oyster sauce
1 tbsp light soy sauce
2 tsp clear honey
1 tsp cornflour
a pinch of salt

1 First, make the sauce. Put all the ingredients in a blender and blend until smooth. Set aside.

2 Drain the tofu, pat it dry and cut it into large cubes. Heat the vegetable oil in a deep-fryer to 180°C (test by frying a small cube of bread; it should brown in 30 seconds). Add the tofu and deep-fry for 1–2 minutes until golden. Drain on kitchen paper.

3 Heat 2 tbsp oil in a wok or large frying pan, add the garlic and fry for 1 minute. Remove the garlic with a slotted spoon and discard. Add the pepper, broccoli and beans to the oil in the pan and stir-fry for 3 minutes. Add the bean sprouts, mushrooms and water chestnuts and stir-fry for a further 1 minute.

4 Add the tofu and sauce to pan and simmer, covered, for 3–4 minutes. Garnish with sprigs of coriander and serve immediately.

Try Something Different

Instead of oyster sauce, use black bean sauce and omit the soy sauce and honey.

Serves 4	A LITTLE EFFORT		NUTRITIONAL INFORMATION	
	Preparation Time 20 minutes	**Cooking Time** about 10 minutes	**Per Serving** 157 calories, 9g fat (of which 1g saturates), 11g carbohydrate, 1.1g salt	Dairy free

Tofu Noodle Curry

250g (9oz) firm tofu

2 tbsp light soy sauce

½ red chilli, chopped (see page 36)

5cm (2in) piece fresh root ginger, peeled and grated

1 tbsp olive oil

1 onion, thinly sliced

2 tbsp Thai red curry paste

200ml (7fl oz) coconut milk

900ml (1½ pints) hot vegetable stock

200g (7oz) baby sweetcorn, halved lengthways

200g (7oz) fine green beans, trimmed

250g (9oz) medium rice noodles

salt and ground black pepper

2 spring onions, sliced diagonally, fresh coriander sprigs and 1 lime, cut into wedges, to garnish

1 Drain the tofu, pat it dry and cut it into large cubes. Put the tofu in a large shallow bowl with the soy sauce, chilli and ginger. Toss well to coat, then set aside to marinate for 30 minutes.

2 Heat the oil in a wok or large frying pan, then add the onion and fry over a medium heat for 10 minutes, stirring, until golden. Add the curry paste and cook for 2 minutes.

3 Add the marinated tofu, coconut milk, stock and sweetcorn and season with salt and pepper. Bring to the boil, then add the green beans. Reduce the heat and simmer for 8–10 minutes.

4 Meanwhile, put the noodles in a large heatproof bowl, pour over boiling water to cover and soak for 30 seconds. Drain, then stir the noodles into the curry. Pour the curry into four serving bowls and garnish with the spring onions, coriander and lime wedges. Serve immediately.

Try Something Different

Use mangetouts or sugarsnap peas instead of green beans.

Add a handful of baby spinach leaves; stir into the curry with the noodles, just before serving.

EASY		NUTRITIONAL INFORMATION		Serves
Preparation Time 15 minutes, plus 30 minutes marinating	**Cooking Time** about 25 minutes	**Per Serving** 367 calories, 7g fat (of which 1g saturates), 60g carbohydrate, 2g salt	Dairy free	**4**

Try Something Different

Braised aubergines: omit the cumin, coriander, cloves, cinnamon and paprika. Add the aubergines to the onion mixture at the end of step 1 and stir-fry for 1–2 minutes. Add 1 tbsp sugar, 1 tsp salt, 3–4 tbsp yellow bean sauce and the water; complete the recipe.

Aubergines in a Hot Sweet and Sour Sauce

3 tbsp vegetable oil

200g (7oz) onions, thinly sliced

2.5cm (1in) piece fresh root ginger, peeled and finely chopped

2 red chillies, finely chopped (see page 36), plus extra whole red chillies to garnish (optional)

1½ tsp cumin seeds

1½ tsp coriander seeds

3 cloves

5cm (2in) cinnamon stick

1 tbsp paprika

juice of 2 limes

3–4 tbsp dark muscovado sugar

1–2 tsp salt

450g (1lb) aubergines, cut into 2.5cm (1in) pieces

rice to serve

1 Heat the oil in a wok or large frying pan, add the onions, ginger and chillies and stir-fry for about 4 minutes until softened. Add the cumin and coriander seeds, cloves and cinnamon and cook for 2–3 minutes.

2 Add 300ml (½ pint) water to the pan, then stir in the paprika, lime juice, sugar, salt and aubergines. Bring to the boil, then simmer, covered, for about 20 minutes until the aubergine is tender.

3 Uncover the pan and bring the sauce back to the boil. Bubble for 3–4 minutes until the liquid is thick enough to coat the aubergine pieces. Serve with rice, garnished with whole red chillies if you like.

Serves 4	EASY		NUTRITIONAL INFORMATION	
	Preparation Time 10 minutes	**Cooking Time** 35 minutes	**Per Serving** 136 calories, 7g fat (of which 1g saturates), 17g carbohydrate, 2.5g salt	Vegetarian Gluten free • Dairy free

Cook's Tip

Banana leaves are sometimes used instead of plates in South-east Asia; they make an unusual presentation and are available from some Asian food shops.

2 tbsp sesame seeds

2 tbsp vegetable oil

4 garlic cloves, crushed

900g (2lb) courgettes, thinly sliced

1 spring onion, thickly sliced

$\frac{1}{2}$ tsp salt

1 tbsp sesame oil

ground black pepper

banana leaves to serve (optional, see Cook's Tip)

Courgettes with Sesame Seeds

1 Toast the sesame seeds in a hot wok or large frying pan until golden. Tip on to a plate.

2 Heat the vegetable oil in the wok or frying pan. Add the garlic and fry for 2 minutes.

3 Add the courgettes and stir-fry for 7–8 minutes. Stir in the spring onion, salt and sesame oil. Season to taste with pepper. Cook for a further 1 minute, then add the toasted sesame seeds. Stir once and serve hot or cold on a bed of banana leaves, if you like.

EASY		NUTRITIONAL INFORMATION		Serves
Preparation Time 5 minutes	**Cooking Time** 12 minutes	**Per Serving** 107 calories, 9g fat (of which 1g saturates), 3g carbohydrate, 0.4g salt	Vegetarian Gluten free • Dairy free	**6**

Cook's Tip

Grow your own bean sprouts for this recipe following the technique on page 23.

Bean Sprouts with Peppers and Chillies

3 tbsp vegetable oil

2 garlic cloves, chopped

2.5cm (1in) piece fresh root ginger, peeled and chopped

6 spring onions, cut into 2.5cm (1in) pieces

1 red pepper, seeded and thinly sliced

1 yellow pepper, seeded and thinly sliced

2 green chillies, seeded and finely chopped (see page 36)

350g (12oz) bean sprouts

1 tbsp dark soy sauce

1 tbsp sugar

1 tbsp malt vinegar

a few drops of sesame oil (optional)

boiled rice with 2 tbsp freshly chopped coriander stirred through to serve

1 Heat the oil in a wok or large frying pan. Add the garlic, ginger, spring onions, peppers, chillies and bean sprouts and stir-fry over a medium heat for 3 minutes.

2 Add the soy sauce, sugar and vinegar and fry, stirring, for a further 1 minute.

3 Sprinkle with a few drops of sesame oil, if you like, then serve immediately with coriander rice.

Serves 4	EASY		NUTRITIONAL INFORMATION	
	Preparation Time 10 minutes	**Cooking Time** 4 minutes	**Per Serving** 149 calories, 9g fat (of which 1g saturates), 14g carbohydrate, 0.7g salt	Vegetarian • Dairy free

Try Something Different

Chinese Garlic Mushrooms: replace the nuts with 2 garlic cloves, crushed, and stir-fry for only 20 seconds before adding the mushrooms. Replace the lemon juice with rice wine or dry sherry.

Mushrooms with Cashew Nuts

1 tbsp vegetable oil

25g (1oz) unsalted cashew nuts

225g (8oz) brown-cap mushrooms, sliced

1 tbsp lemon juice

4 tbsp freshly chopped coriander, plus fresh sprigs to garnish

1 tbsp single cream (optional)

salt and ground black pepper

1 Heat the oil in a wok or large frying pan. Add the cashew nuts and cook over a high heat for 2–3 minutes until golden. Add the mushrooms and cook for a further 2–3 minutes until tender, stirring frequently.

2 Stir in the lemon juice and coriander and season to taste with salt and pepper. Heat until bubbling. Remove the pan from the heat and stir in the cream, if using. Adjust the seasoning if necessary, and serve immediately, garnished with coriander sprigs.

EASY		NUTRITIONAL INFORMATION		Serves
Preparation Time 5 minutes	**Cooking Time** 5–8 minutes	**Per Serving** 75 calories, 6g fat (of which 1g saturates), 2g carbohydrate, 0.1g salt	Vegetarian • Gluten free	**4**

Sesame and Cabbage Rolls

50g (2oz) dried shiitake mushrooms

3 tbsp sesame oil

4 garlic cloves, crushed

4 tbsp sesame seeds

450g (1lb) cabbage, finely shredded

1 bunch of spring onions, trimmed and chopped

225g can bamboo shoots, drained

3 tbsp soy sauce

1/2 tsp caster sugar

2 x 270g packs filo pastry

1 large egg, beaten

vegetable oil for deep-frying

Spiced Plum Sauce or Thai Chilli Dipping Sauce to serve
(see Cook's Tip)

1   Put the mushrooms in a heatproof bowl and cover with boiling water. Soak for 20 minutes.

2   Heat the sesame oil in a wok or large frying pan. Add the garlic and sesame seeds and fry gently until golden brown. Add the cabbage and spring onions and fry, stirring, for 3 minutes.

3   Drain and slice the mushrooms. Add them to the pan with the bamboo shoots, soy sauce and sugar and stir until well mixed. Remove the pan from the heat and leave to cool.

4   Cut the filo pastry into 24 x 18cm (7in) squares. Keep the filo squares covered with a damp teatowel as you work. Place one square of filo pastry on the worksurface and cover with a second square. Place a heaped tablespoon of the cabbage mixture across the centre of the top square to within 2.5cm (1in) of the ends. Fold the 2.5cm (1in) ends of pastry over the filling. Brush one unfolded edge of the pastry with a little beaten egg, then roll up to make a thick parcel shape. Shape the remaining pastry and filling in the same way to make 12 parcels.

5   Heat a 5cm (2in) depth of oil in a deep-fryer or large heavy-based saucepan to 180°C (test by frying a small cube of bread; it should brown in 30 seconds). Fry the rolls in batches for about 3 minutes or until crisp and golden. Remove with a slotted spoon and drain on kitchen paper; keep them warm while you fry the remainder. Serve hot with a sauce for dipping.

Cook's Tip

Spiced Plum Sauce: slice 2 spring onions as thinly as possible. Put them in a small pan with 6 tbsp plum sauce, the juice of 1 lime, 1/2 tsp Chinese five-spice powder and 2 tbsp water. Heat gently for 2 minutes.

Thai Chilli Dipping Sauce: put 200ml (7fl oz) white wine vinegar and 6 tbsp caster sugar in a small pan, bring to the boil and simmer for 2 minutes. Add 1 finely chopped red chilli and 50g (2oz) each finely chopped cucumber, onion and pineapple.

Makes 12	A LITTLE EFFORT		NUTRITIONAL INFORMATION	
	Preparation Time 30 minutes, plus soaking and cooling	**Cooking Time** about 15 minutes	**Per Roll** 224 calories, 13g fat (of which 2g saturates), 23g carbohydrate, 0.7g salt	Vegetarian • Dairy free

Try Something Different

This serves four with other dishes as part of a Chinese meal, but for a quick (non-vegetarian) supper for two, add 75g (3oz) cooked peeled prawns.

Egg Fu Yung

3 tbsp groundnut or vegetable oil

8 spring onions, finely sliced, plus extra spring onion curls to garnish (see Cook's Tip, page 47)

125g (4oz) shiitake or oyster mushrooms, sliced

125g (4oz) canned bamboo shoots, drained and chopped

1/2 green pepper, seeded and finely chopped

125g (4oz) frozen peas, thawed

6 medium eggs, beaten

2 good pinches of chilli powder

1 tbsp light soy sauce

a pinch of salt

1 Heat the oil in a wok or large frying pan, add the spring onions, mushrooms, bamboo shoots, green pepper and peas and stir-fry for 2–3 minutes.

2 Season the eggs with salt and chilli powder. Pour the eggs into the pan and continue to cook, stirring, until the egg mixture is set.

3 Sprinkle over the soy sauce and stir well. Serve immediately, garnished with spring onion curls.

Serves 4	EASY		NUTRITIONAL INFORMATION	
	Preparation Time 10 minutes	**Cooking Time** about 5 minutes	**Per Serving** 232 calories, 18g fat (of which 4g saturates), 6g carbohydrate, 0.9g salt	Vegetarian • Dairy free

▼ **Vegetable Tempura**
▶ **Steamed Sesame Salmon** (see page 47)
▶ **Stir-fried Green Vegetables** (see page 93)

125g (4oz) plain flour, plus 2 tbsp extra to sprinkle

2 tbsp cornflour

2 tbsp arrowroot

125g (4oz) cauliflower, cut into small florets

2 large carrots, cut into matchsticks

16 button mushrooms

2 courgettes, sliced

2 red peppers, seeded and sliced

vegetable oil for deep-frying

salt and ground black pepper

fresh coriander sprigs to garnish

For the dipping sauce

25g (1oz) fresh root ginger, peeled and grated

4 tbsp dry sherry

3 tbsp soy sauce

Vegetable Tempura

1 Sift 125g (4oz) flour, the cornflour and arrowroot into a large bowl with a pinch each of salt and pepper. Gradually whisk in 300ml (½ pint) ice-cold water to form a thin batter. Cover and chill.

2 To make the dipping sauce, put the ginger, sherry and soy sauce in a heatproof bowl and pour over 200ml (7fl oz) boiling water. Stir well to mix, then set aside.

3 Put the vegetables in a large bowl and sprinkle over 2 tbsp flour. Toss well to coat. Heat the oil in a wok or deep-fryer to 170°C (test by frying a small cube of bread; it should brown in 40 seconds).

4 Dip a handful of the vegetables in the batter, then remove with a slotted spoon, taking up a lot of the batter with the vegetables. Add to the hot oil and deep-fry for 3–5 minutes until crisp and golden. Remove with a slotted spoon and drain on kitchen paper; keep them hot while you cook the remaining batches. Serve immediately, garnished with coriander sprigs and accompanied by the dipping sauce.

A LITTLE EFFORT		NUTRITIONAL INFORMATION		Serves
Preparation Time 20 minutes	**Cooking Time** 15 minutes	**Per Serving** 450 calories, 21g fat (of which 3g saturates), 55g carbohydrate, 2.1g salt	Vegetarian • Dairy free	**4**

5

Rice and Noodles

Simple Fried Rice

150g (5oz) long-grain rice
2 tbsp sesame oil
3 medium eggs, lightly beaten
250g (9oz) frozen petits pois
250g (9oz) cooked peeled prawns

1 Cook the rice in boiling water for about 10 minutes or according to the packet instructions. Drain well.

2 Heat 1 tsp sesame oil in a large non-stick frying pan. Pour in half the beaten eggs and tilt the pan around over the heat for about 1 minute until the egg is set. Tip the omelette on to a warm plate. Repeat with another 1 tsp sesame oil and the remaining beaten egg to make another omelette. Tip on to another warm plate.

3 Add the remaining oil to the pan and stir in the rice and peas. Stir-fry for 2–3 minutes until the peas are cooked. Stir in the prawns.

4 Roll up the omelettes, roughly chop one-third of one, then slice the remainder into strips. Add the chopped omelette to the rice, peas and prawns, and cook for 1–2 minutes until heated through. Divide the fried rice among four serving bowls, top with the sliced omelette and serve immediately.

| | EASY | | NUTRITIONAL INFORMATION | |
| Serves 4 | **Preparation Time** 5 minutes | **Cooking Time** 15–20 minutes | **Per Serving** 339 calories, 11g fat (of which 2g saturates), 37g carbohydrate, 0.4g salt | Gluten free • Dairy free |

- Egg Fu Yung (see page 106)
- Twice-cooked Pork with Black Bean Sauce (see page 73)
- Rice and Red Pepper Stir-fry

Rice and Red Pepper Stir-fry

75g (3oz) long-grain rice

200ml (7fl oz) hot vegetable stock

1/2 onion, thinly sliced

2 rashers of streaky bacon, chopped

1 small red pepper, seeded and cut into chunks

2 tsp vegetable oil

a handful of frozen peas

a dash of Worcestershire sauce

1 Put the rice in a pan and pour over the hot stock. Cover, bring to the boil and simmer for 10 minutes or until the rice is tender and the liquid has been absorbed.

2 Meanwhile, heat the oil in a wok or large frying pan over a medium heat. Add the onion and fry for 5 minutes. Add the bacon and pepper and fry for a further 5 minutes or until the bacon is crisp.

3 Stir the cooked rice and the peas into the onion mixture and cook, stirring occasionally, for 2–3 minutes until the rice and peas are hot. Add a dash of Worcestershire sauce and serve immediately.

EASY		NUTRITIONAL INFORMATION		Serves
Preparation Time 5 minutes	**Cooking Time** 15 minutes	**Per Serving** 157 calories, 5g fat (of which 1g saturates), 22g carbohydrate, 0.5g salt	Gluten free • Dairy free	4

Vegetable Fried Rice

200g (7oz) long-grain rice

3 Chinese dried mushrooms, or 125g (4oz) button mushrooms, sliced

2 tbsp vegetable oil

4 spring onions, sliced diagonally into 2.5cm (1in) lengths

125g (4oz) canned bamboo shoots, drained and cut into 2.5cm (1in) strips

125g (4oz) bean sprouts

125g (4oz) frozen peas

2 tbsp soy sauce

3 medium eggs, beaten

fresh coriander sprigs to garnish

1 Put the rice in a pan, cover with enough cold water to come 2.5cm (1in) above the rice, bring to the boil, cover tightly and simmer very gently for 20 minutes. Do not stir.

2 Remove the pan from the heat, leave to cool for 20 minutes, then cover with clingfilm and chill for 2–3 hours or overnight.

3 When ready to fry the rice, soak the dried mushrooms, if using, in warm water for about 30 minutes.

4 Drain the mushrooms, squeeze out excess moisture, then thinly slice.

5 Heat the oil in a wok or large frying pan over a high heat. Add the mushrooms, spring onions, bamboo shoots, bean sprouts and peas and stir-fry for 2–3 minutes. Add the soy sauce and cook briefly, stirring.

6 Fork up the rice, add it to the pan and stir-fry for 2 minutes. Pour in the eggs and continue to stir-fry for 2–3 minutes until the egg has scrambled and the rice is heated through. Serve immediately, garnished with coriander.

EASY		NUTRITIONAL INFORMATION		Serves
Preparation Time 10 minutes, plus soaking and chilling	**Cooking Time** about 30 minutes	**Per Serving** 464 calories, 11g fat (of which 2g saturates), 76g carbohydrate, 1.5g salt	Vegetarian • Dairy free	**4**

Cook's Tip

Nasi goreng is a spicy Indonesian dish traditionally eaten for breakfast. Nasi goreng paste can be bought at large supermarkets and Asian food shops.

If you can't find microwave rice, use 200g (7oz) long-grain rice, cooked according to the packet instructions – but do not overcook. Rinse in cold water and drain well before you begin the recipe.

1 tbsp sesame oil

6 tbsp nasi goreng paste

200g (7oz) green cabbage, shredded

250g (9oz) cooked peeled large prawns

2 x 250g packs of microwave rice

2 tbsp light soy sauce

1 tbsp sunflower oil

2 medium eggs, beaten

2 spring onions, thinly sliced

1 lime, cut into wedges, to serve

Special Prawn Fried Rice

1 Heat the sesame oil in a wok and fry the nasi goreng paste for 1–2 minutes. Add the cabbage and stir-fry for 2–3 minutes. Add the prawns and stir briefly, then add the rice and soy sauce and cook for a further 5 minutes, stirring occasionally.

2 To make the omelette, heat the sunflower oil in a non-stick frying pan (about 25.5cm/10in in diameter) and add the eggs. Swirl around to cover the base of the pan in a thin layer and cook for 2–3 minutes until set.

3 Roll up the omelette and cut it into strips. Serve the rice scattered with the omelette and spring onions, and pass around the lime wedges to squeeze over.

Serves 4	EASY		NUTRITIONAL INFORMATION	
	Preparation Time 5 minutes	**Cooking Time** 10–13 minutes	**Per Serving** 412 calories, 18g fat (of which 3g saturates), 46g carbohydrate, 1.9g salt	Dairy free

Thai Egg Noodles

1 lemongrass stalk, inner leaves only, finely chopped

100g (3½oz) medium egg noodles

100g (3½oz) sugarsnap peas, halved diagonally

4 tbsp vegetable oil

4 garlic cloves, crushed

3 large eggs, beaten

juice of 2 lemons

3 tbsp Thai fish sauce

2 tbsp light soy sauce

½ tsp caster sugar

50g (2oz) roasted salted peanuts

½ tsp chilli powder

12 spring onions, roughly chopped

150g (5oz) bean sprouts

2 tbsp freshly chopped coriander, plus extra to garnish

salt and ground black pepper

1 Put the lemongrass in a heatproof bowl with the noodles. Pour over 600ml (1 pint) boiling water and set aside for 20 minutes, stirring from time to time.

2 Cook the sugarsnap peas in salted boiling water for 1 minute, then drain and plunge them into ice-cold water.

3 Heat the oil in a wok or large frying pan, add the garlic and fry for 30 seconds. Add the beaten eggs and cook gently until lightly scrambled. Add the lemon juice, fish sauce, soy sauce, sugar, peanuts, chilli powder, spring onions and bean sprouts to the eggs. Pour the noodles, lemongrass and soaking liquid into the pan. Bring to the boil and bubble for 4–5 minutes, stirring from time to time.

4 Drain the sugarsnap peas, then add them to the noodle mixture with the chopped coriander. Heat through and season with salt and pepper. Garnish with coriander and serve immediately.

EASY		NUTRITIONAL INFORMATION		Serves
Preparation Time 15 minutes, plus 20 minutes soaking	**Cooking Time** 12–15 minutes	**Per Serving** 289 calories, 18g fat (of which 3g saturates), 24g carbohydrate, 2.9g salt	Dairy free	**4**

Try Something Different

Use chicken, cut into thin strips, instead of the prawns.

Yellow Bean Noodles with Tiger Prawns

250g (9oz) medium egg noodles

1 tbsp stir-fry oil or sesame oil

1 garlic clove, sliced

1 tsp freshly grated root ginger

1 bunch of spring onions, each cut into four

250g (9oz) raw peeled tiger prawns, thawed if frozen

200g (7oz) pak choi, leaves separated and white base cut into thick slices

160g jar Chinese yellow bean stir-fry sauce

1 Put the noodles in a large heatproof bowl and pour over 2 litres (3½ pints) boiling water. Leave to soak for 4 minutes. Drain and set aside.

2 Heat the oil in a wok or large frying pan. Add the garlic and ginger, then stir-fry for 30 seconds. Add the spring onions and prawns and cook for 2 minutes.

3 Boil the kettle. Add the sliced white pak choi stems to the pan with the yellow bean sauce. Fill the sauce jar with boiling water, pour it into the pan and stir well to mix.

4 Add the drained noodles to the pan and cook for 1 minute, tossing every now and then, until heated through. Stir in the pak choi leaves and serve immediately.

Serves 4	EASY		NUTRITIONAL INFORMATION	
	Preparation Time 10 minutes, plus 4 minutes soaking	**Cooking Time** 5 minutes	**Per Serving** 403 calories, 10g fat (of which 2g saturates), 62g carbohydrate, 0.7g salt	Dairy free

Cook's Tip

Laksa paste is a hot and spicy paste; you could use Thai curry paste instead.

1 tbsp olive oil

1 onion, thinly sliced

3 tbsp laksa paste (see Cook's Tip)

200ml (7fl oz) coconut milk

900ml (1½ pints) hot vegetable stock

200g (7oz) baby sweetcorn, halved lengthways

600g (1lb 5oz) piece skinless salmon fillet, cut into 1cm (½in) slices

225g (8oz) baby leaf spinach, washed

250g (9oz) medium rice noodles

salt and ground black pepper

2 spring onions, sliced diagonally, 2 tbsp freshly chopped coriander and 1 lime, cut into wedges, to garnish

Salmon Laksa Curry

1 Heat the oil in a wok or large frying pan, then add the onion and fry over a medium heat for 10 minutes, stirring, until golden. Add the laksa paste and cook for 2 minutes.

2 Add the coconut milk, stock and baby corn and season with salt and pepper. Bring to the boil, reduce the heat and simmer for 5 minutes.

3 Add the salmon slices and spinach, stirring to immerse them in the liquid. Cook for 4 minutes until the fish is opaque all the way through.

4 Meanwhile, put the noodles in a large heatproof bowl, pour over boiling water to cover and soak for 30 seconds. Drain well, then stir them into the curry. Pour the curry into four serving bowls and garnish with the spring onions, coriander and lime wedges. Serve immediately.

EASY		NUTRITIONAL INFORMATION		Serves
Preparation Time 10 minutes	**Cooking Time** about 20 minutes	**Per Serving** 570 calories, 22g fat (of which 3g saturates), 55g carbohydrate, 1.9g salt	Gluten free • Dairy free	**4**

Thai Noodles with Tofu

125g (4oz) firm tofu, drained and cut into 2.5cm (1in) cubes

8 shallots, halved

1 garlic clove, crushed

2.5cm (1in) piece fresh root ginger, peeled and grated

2 tbsp soy sauce

1 tsp rice vinegar

225g (8oz) rice noodles

25g (1oz) unsalted peanuts

2 tbsp sunflower oil

15g (½oz) dried shrimp (optional)

1 medium egg, beaten

25g (1oz) bean sprouts

fresh basil leaves to garnish

For the sauce

1 dried red chilli, seeded and finely chopped

2 tbsp lemon juice

1 tbsp Thai fish sauce

1 tbsp caster sugar

2 tbsp smooth peanut butter

1 Preheat the oven to 200°C (180°C fan oven) mark 6. Put the tofu and shallots in a small roasting pan. Put the garlic, ginger, soy sauce, vinegar and 2 tbsp water in a bowl and stir well. Pour the mixture over the tofu and shallots and toss well to coat. Roast near the top of the oven for 30 minutes until the tofu and shallots are golden.

2 Meanwhile, soak the noodles according to the packet instructions. Drain, refresh under cold running water and set aside. Toast and chop the peanuts.

3 To make the sauce, put all the ingredients in a small pan and stir over a gentle heat until the sugar dissolves. Keep the sauce warm.

4 Heat the oil in a wok or large frying pan and stir-fry the dried shrimp, if using, for 1 minute. Add the drained noodles and beaten egg to the pan and stir over a medium heat for 3 minutes. Add the tofu and shallots, together with any pan juices. Stir well, then remove from the heat.

5 Stir in the bean sprouts and the sauce, then divide among four warmed serving plates. Sprinkle with the toasted peanuts and serve immediately, garnished with basil leaves.

EASY		NUTRITIONAL INFORMATION		Serves
Preparation Time 25 minutes	**Cooking Time** 35 minutes	**Per Serving** 431 calories, 15g fat (of which 3g saturates), 61g carbohydrate, 2.1g salt	Dairy free	**4**

Cook's Tip

If you can't find satay and sweet chilli pesto, substitute 2 tbsp peanut butter and 1 tbsp sweet chilli sauce. Chilli soy sauce can be replaced with 2 tbsp light soy sauce and ½ red chilli, finely chopped (see page 36).

250g (9oz) wide ribbon rice noodles

3 tbsp satay and sweet chilli pesto

125g (4oz) mangetouts, thinly sliced

125g (4oz) sugarsnap peas, thinly sliced

3 medium eggs, beaten

3 tbsp chilli soy sauce, plus extra to serve

250g (9oz) cooked peeled tiger prawns

25g (1oz) dry-roasted peanuts, roughly crushed

lime wedges to serve (optional)

Quick Pad Thai

1 Put the noodles in a heatproof bowl, cover with boiling water and soak for 4 minutes until softened. Drain, rinse under cold water and set aside.

2 Heat a wok or large frying pan until hot, add the chilli pesto and stir-fry for 1 minute. Add the mangetouts and sugarsnap peas and cook for a further 2 minutes. Tip into a bowl. Put the pan back on the heat, add the eggs and cook, stirring, for 1 minute.

3 Add the soy sauce, prawns and noodles to the pan. Toss well and cook for 3 minutes until piping hot. Return the vegetables to the pan, cook for a further 1 minute until heated through, then sprinkle with the peanuts. Serve with extra soy sauce and lime wedges to squeeze over, if you like.

Serves	EASY		NUTRITIONAL INFORMATION	
4	**Preparation Time** 12 minutes, plus 4 minutes soaking	**Cooking Time** 8 minutes	**Per Serving** 451 calories, 13g fat (of which 3g saturates), 56g carbohydrate, 2.6g salt	Dairy free

Pork and Noodle Stir-fry

1 tbsp sesame oil

5cm (2in) piece fresh root ginger, peeled and grated

2 tbsp soy sauce

1 tbsp fish sauce

½ red chilli, finely chopped (see page 36)

450g (1lb) stir-fry pork strips

2 red peppers, seeded and roughly chopped

250g (9oz) baby sweetcorn, halved lengthways

200g (7oz) sugarsnap peas, halved

300g (11oz) bean sprouts

250g (9oz) rice noodles

1 Put the sesame oil in a large bowl. Add the ginger, soy sauce, fish sauce, chilli and pork strips. Mix well and leave to marinate for 10 minutes.

2 Heat a wok or large frying pan until hot. Lift the pork out of the marinade with a slotted spoon and add it to the pan. Stir-fry over a high heat for 5 minutes. Add the peppers, sweetcorn, sugarsnap peas, bean sprouts and remaining marinade and stir-fry for a further 2–3 minutes until the pork is cooked.

3 Meanwhile, soak the noodles for 4 minutes or according to the packet instructions.

4 Drain the noodles, add them to the pan and toss well. Serve immediately.

EASY		NUTRITIONAL INFORMATION		Serves
Preparation Time 15 minutes, plus marinating	**Cooking Time** 7–8 minutes	**Per Serving** 476 calories, 8g fat (of which 2g saturates), 64g carbohydrate, 3.4g salt	Dairy free	**4**

Chicken Chow Mein

250g (9oz) medium egg noodles
1 tbsp toasted sesame oil
2 skinless chicken breast fillets, cut into thin strips
a bunch of spring onions, thinly sliced diagonally
150g (5oz) mangetouts, thickly sliced diagonally
125g (4oz) bean sprouts
100g (3½ oz) cooked ham, finely shredded
120g sachet chow mein sauce
salt and ground black pepper
light soy sauce to serve

1 Cook the noodles in boiling water for 4 minutes or according to the packet instructions. Drain, rinse thoroughly in cold water, drain and set aside.

2 Meanwhile, heat a wok or large frying pan until hot, then add the oil. Add the chicken and stir-fry over a high heat for 3–4 minutes until browned all over. Add the spring onions and mangetouts, stir-fry for 2 minutes, then stir in the bean sprouts and ham and cook for a further 2 minutes.

3 Add the drained noodles, then pour over the chow mein sauce and toss together to coat evenly. Stir-fry for 2 minutes or until piping hot. Season with salt and pepper and serve immediately with light soy sauce to drizzle over.

Serves 4	EASY		NUTRITIONAL INFORMATION	
	Preparation Time 10 minutes	**Cooking Time** 10 minutes	**Per Serving** 451 calories, 11g fat (of which 2g saturates), 59g carbohydrate, 1.3g salt	Dairy free

▶ **Scallops with Ginger** (see page 33)
▶ **Crispy Duck with Mangetouts**
  (see page 67)
▼ **Beef Chow Mein**

2 tsp dark soy sauce

4 tsp dry sherry

1 tsp cornflour

1 tsp sugar

1 tbsp sesame oil

225g (8oz) rump steak, cut into thin strips about
7.5cm (3in) long

175g (6oz) egg noodles

3 tbsp vegetable oil

1 bunch of spring onions, sliced

3 garlic cloves, crushed

1 large green chilli, sliced (see page 36)

125g (4oz) Chinese leaves, or cabbage, sliced

50g (2oz) bean sprouts

salt and ground black pepper

Beef Chow Mein

1 Put the soy sauce, sherry, cornflour, sugar and 1 tsp sesame oil in a bowl and whisk together. Pour this mixture over the beef. Cover and marinate in the refrigerator for at least 1 hour or overnight.

2 Cook the noodles for 4 minutes or according to the packet instructions. Rinse in cold water and drain.

3 Drain the beef, reserving the marinade. Heat the vegetable oil in a wok or large, non-stick frying pan and fry the beef over a high heat until well browned. Remove with a slotted spoon and set aside.

4 Add the spring onions, garlic, chilli, Chinese leaves and bean sprouts to the pan and stir-fry for 2–3 minutes. Return the beef to the pan with the noodles and reserved marinade. Bring to the boil, stirring all the time, and bubble for 2–3 minutes. Sprinkle over the remaining sesame oil, season with salt and pepper and serve immediately.

EASY		NUTRITIONAL INFORMATION		Serves
Preparation Time 15 minutes, plus marinating	**Cooking Time** 15 minutes	**Per Serving** 408 calories, 20g fat (of which 5g saturates), 38g carbohydrate, 1.2g salt	Dairy free	**4**

Mee Goreng

125g (4oz) rump steak, very thinly sliced across the grain

2 garlic cloves

2 tbsp soy sauce

450g (1lb) cleaned squid

225g (8oz) egg noodles

1 tbsp vegetable oil

1 tbsp sesame oil

1–2 hot red chillies, chopped (see page 36)

2.5cm (1in) piece fresh root ginger, peeled and finely chopped

2–3 spring onions, sliced

175g (6oz) large raw peeled prawns, deveined

2 tbsp hoisin sauce

1 tbsp lemon juice

2 tbsp Thai fish sauce

125g (4oz) bean sprouts

1 medium egg, beaten

lemon wedges to serve

1 Put the steak in a shallow dish with 1 garlic clove and 1 tbsp soy sauce. Leave to stand.

2 Wash and dry the squid. Cut the tentacles into small pieces. Open out the body pouches and cut into small rectangular pieces.

3 Put the noodles in a large heatproof bowl and pour over plenty of boiling water. Leave to soak for about 4 minutes or according to the packet instructions.

4 Heat the vegetable and sesame oils in a wok or large frying pan, add the remaining garlic, the chillies, ginger and spring onions and cook for 2 minutes, stirring all the time.

5 Add the beef and cook for 2 minutes. Add the squid and prawns and cook for 2 minutes. Add the hoisin sauce, lemon juice, fish sauce and remaining soy sauce and cook for 2 minutes.

6 Drain the noodles and add them to the pan with the bean sprouts. Cook for a couple of minutes until heated through, then add the beaten egg. Cook briefly until the egg is on the point of setting. Serve immediately, with lemon wedges to squeeze over.

Try Something Different

For a less elaborate version of this Malaysian dish, omit the squid and replace the raw prawns with 225g (8oz) cooked peeled prawns.

Serves 6	A LITTLE EFFORT		NUTRITIONAL INFORMATION	
	Preparation Time 30 minutes	**Cooking Time** about 12 minutes	**Per Serving** 306 calories, 11g fat (of which 3g saturates), 31g carbohydrate, 2g salt	Dairy free

vegetable oil for deep-frying

125g (4oz) rice or egg noodles

frisée leaves to serve

For the sauce

2 tbsp vegetable oil

1 garlic clove, crushed

1cm (½ in) piece fresh root ginger, peeled and grated

6 spring onions, sliced

½ red pepper, seeded and finely chopped

2 tbsp sugar

2 tbsp malt vinegar

2 tbsp tomato ketchup

2 tbsp dark soy sauce

2 tbsp dry sherry

1 tbsp cornflour

1 tbsp sliced green chillies (see page 36)

Crispy Noodles with Hot Sweet and Sour Sauce

1 First, make the sauce. Heat the oil in a wok or large frying pan and stir-fry the garlic, ginger, spring onions and red pepper for 1 minute. Stir in the sugar, vinegar, ketchup, soy sauce and sherry. Blend the cornflour with 8 tbsp water and stir it into the sauce. Cook for 2 minutes, stirring. Add the chillies, cover and keep the sauce warm.

2 Heat the vegetable oil in a deep-fryer to 190°C (test by frying a small cube of bread; it should brown in 20 seconds). Cut the noodles into six portions and fry, a batch at a time, very briefly until lightly golden (take care as the hot oil rises up quickly).

3 Drain the noodles on kitchen paper and keep them warm while you cook the remainder.

4 Arrange the noodles on a bed of frisée leaves and serve immediately with the sauce served separately.

Serves 4	A LITTLE EFFORT		NUTRITIONAL INFORMATION	
	Preparation Time 10 minutes	**Cooking Time** about 15 minutes	**Per Serving** 317 calories, 14g fat (of which 2g saturates), 43g carbohydrate, 1.7g salt	Vegetarian • Dairy free

Glossary

Al dente Italian term commonly used to describe foods, especially pasta and vegetables, which are cooked until tender but still firm to the bite.

Baste To spoon the juices and melted fat over meat, poultry, game or vegetables during roasting to keep them moist. The term is also used to describe spooning over a marinade.

Beat To incorporate air into an ingredient or mixture by agitating it vigorously with a spoon, fork, whisk or electric mixer.

Blanch To immerse food briefly in fast-boiling water to loosen skins, such as peaches or tomatoes, or to remove bitterness, or to destroy enzymes and preserve the colour, flavour and texture of vegetables (especially prior to freezing).

Bouquet garni Small bunch of herbs – usually a mixture of parsley stems, thyme and a bay leaf – tied in muslin and used to flavour stocks, soups and stews.

Chill To cool food in the fridge.

Crudités Raw vegetables, usually cut into slices or sticks, typically served with a dipping sauce.

Curdle To cause sauces or creamed mixtures to separate, usually by overheating or over-beating.

Cure To preserve fish, meat or poultry by smoking, drying or salting.

Deglaze To heat stock, wine or other liquid with the cooking juices left in the pan after roasting or sautéeing, scraping and stirring vigorously to dissolve the sediment on the bottom of the pan.

Dice To cut food into small cubes.

Dust To sprinkle lightly with flour, cornflour, icing sugar etc.

Escalope Thin slice of meat, such as pork, veal or turkey, from the top of the leg, usually pan-fried.

Fillet Term used to describe boned breasts of birds, boned sides of fish, and the undercut of a loin of beef, lamb, pork or veal.

Flake To separate food, such as cooked fish, into natural pieces.

Fry To cook food in hot fat or oil. There are various methods: shallow-frying in a little fat in a shallow pan; deep-frying where the food is totally immersed in oil; dry-frying in which fatty foods are cooked in a non-stick pan without extra fat; see also Stir-frying.

Garnish A decoration, usually edible, such as parsley or lemon, which is used to enhance the appearance of a savoury dish.

Gluten A protein constituent of grains, such as wheat and rye, which develops when the flour is mixed with water to give the dough elasticity. Some people are allergic to or intolerant of gluten in their food and have to avoid eating it. Wheat is an ingredient of many Chinese sauces, including soy sauce. Gluten-free versions of some sauces are available: tamari is a wheat-free Japanese soy sauce.

Griddle A flat, heavy, metal plate used on the hob for cooking scones or for searing savoury ingredients.

Gut To clean out the entrails from fish.

Infuse To immerse flavourings, such as aromatic vegetables, herbs, spices and vanilla, in a liquid to impart flavour. Usually the infused liquid is brought to the boil, then left to stand for a while.

Julienne Fine 'matchstick' strips of vegetables or citrus zest, sometimes used as a garnish.

Macerate To soften and flavour raw or dried foods by soaking in a liquid, eg soaking fruit in alcohol.

Marinate To soak raw meat, poultry or game – usually in a mixture of oil, wine, vinegar and flavourings – to soften and impart flavour. The mixture, which is known as a marinade, may also be used to baste the food during cooking.

Medallion Small round piece of meat, usually beef or veal.

Mince To cut food into very fine pieces, using a mincer, food processor or knife.

Parboil To boil a vegetable or other food for part of its cooking time before finishing it by another method.

Pare To finely peel the skin or zest from vegetables or fruit.

Poach To cook food gently in liquid at simmering point; the surface should be just trembling.

Pot roast To cook meat in a covered pan with some fat and a little liquid.

Purée To pound, sieve or liquidise vegetables, fish or fruit to a smooth pulp. Purées often form the basis for soups and sauces.

Reduce To fast-boil stock or other liquid in an uncovered pan to evaporate water and concentrate the flavour.

Refresh To cool hot vegetables very quickly by plunging into ice-cold water or holding under cold running water in order to stop the cooking process and preserve the colour.

Roast To cook food by dry heat in the oven.

Salsa Piquant sauce made from chopped fresh vegetables and sometimes fruit.

Sauté To cook food in a small quantity of fat over a high heat, shaking the pan constantly – usually in a sauté pan (a frying pan with straight sides and a wide base).

Scald To pour boiling water over food to clean it, or loosen skin, eg tomatoes. Also used to describe heating milk to just below boiling point.

Score To cut parallel lines in the surface of food, such as fish (or the fat layer on meat), to improve its appearance or help it cook more quickly.

Sear To brown meat quickly in a little hot fat before grilling or roasting.

Seasoned flour Flour mixed with a little salt and pepper, used for dusting meat, fish etc., before frying.

Shred To grate cheese or slice vegetables into very fine pieces or strips.

Sieve To press food through a perforated sieve to obtain a smooth texture.

Sift To shake dry ingredients through a sieve to remove lumps.

Simmer To keep a liquid just below boiling point.

Skim To remove froth, scum or fat from the surface of stock, gravy, stews, jam etc. Use either a skimmer, a spoon or kitchen paper.

Steam To cook food in steam, usually in a steamer over rapidly boiling water.

Steep To immerse food in warm or cold liquid to soften it, and sometimes to draw out strong flavours.

Stew To cook food, such as tougher cuts of meat, in flavoured liquid which is kept at simmering point.

Stir-fry To cook small even-sized pieces of food rapidly in a little fat, tossing constantly over a high heat.

Sweat To cook chopped or sliced vegetables in a little fat without liquid in a covered pan over a low heat to soften.

Tepid The term used to describe temperature at approximately blood heat, ie 37°C (98.7°F).

Zest The thin coloured outer layer of citrus fruit, which can be removed in fine strips with a zester.

Index